30
Pocket Chart Poems That Teach Phonics

by Linda B. Ross

SCHOLASTIC
PROFESSIONAL BOOKS

New York • Toronto • London • Auckland • Sydney
Mexico City • New Delhi • Hong Kong • Buenos Aires

Dedication

To my mother, whose strength and courage
will always inspire me

Cover design by Gerard Fuchs
Cover artwork by Marta Avilés
Interior artwork by Maxie Chambliss
Interior design by Sydney Wright

ISBN: 0-439-22249-4
Copyright © 2003 by Linda B. Ross
All rights reserved. Published by Scholastic Inc.
Printed in the U.S.A.

13 14 15 16 17 18 19   40   13 14 15 16/0

Contents

Introduction

Using *Pocket Chart Poems That Teach Phonics* is as easy as can be! That's because each lesson follows a simple step-by-step plan that makes it a pleasure to teach phonics skills and fun to learn them.

These motivating lessons can be easily folded into your reading instructional plan, whether you use a basal reading program or some combination of methods and materials. You may use the lessons to introduce sound-letter relationships or to practice and review them. It's up to you!

Pocket charts are a wonderful way to teach phonics and language skills. Children are able to actively participate in the learning process by manipulating the words and pictures for the pocket chart poems, as they practice specific sound-letter relationships. After a class activity, the pocket chart poem may be displayed in a learning center to provide independent follow-up activities for small groups and individuals.

How the Book Is Organized

The lesson plans for initial consonants are presented first. They are followed by the lessons for short vowels and long vowels. The next section of the book contains the pictures that are used in each lesson to teach the specific letter-sound relationship.

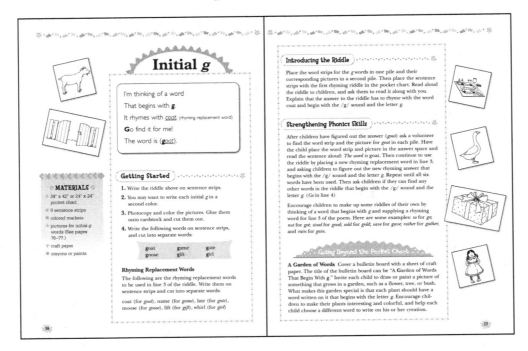

A Look at the Lesson Plan

Materials: All the materials that are needed to carry out the lesson are listed. They will always include a pocket chart, sentence strips, colored markers, and the pictures from pages 68–127 that are used to teach the specific sound-letter relationship. In addition, simple classroom materials, such as crayons and drawing paper, may be listed for carrying out the Going Beyond the Pocket Chart Activity included for each lesson.

Pocket Chart Poem/Riddle: Each lesson plan features a Pocket Chart Poem or Riddle, which utilizes the sound-letter relationship that is the focus of the lesson.

Getting Started: This section explains what you need to do to set up the pocket chart for the lesson.

Word Box: We've listed the words that correspond to the pictures for the targeted sound-letter relationship. In some lessons, other words (Rhyming Replacement Words) will be listed, as well.

Introducing the Poem/Riddle: This first part of the lesson introduces the poem or riddle and the sound-letter relationship that is the focus of the lesson.

Strengthening Phonics Skills: This part of the lesson presents an activity that utilizes the poem or riddle, the pictures from pages 68–127, and the corresponding words.

Going Beyond the Pocket Chart: This part of the lesson presents a fun follow-up activity that gives children the opportunity to practice the sound-letter relationship in a new context. This activity always involves some kind of writing.

Pocket Chart Pointers

Hanging and Displaying Pocket Charts

❋ Position your pocket chart in a location where students will have room to interact with the text and move freely.

❋ Place pocket charts low enough for children to reach all ten rows easily. Consider placing a stepstool nearby for children of all heights to use as they work with the chart.

Storing Sentence Strips

❋ Organize the sentence strips by the skill they help children practice.

❋ Clip each set of strips together with butterfly clips or large paper clips and label them.

❋ Store the sets in a long, under-the-bed storage box. Or, store sentence strips in the box in which they arrived from the vendor.

Resources for Pocket Chart Supplies

❋ Pocket charts and sentence strips are available at most teaching supply stores.

❋ They may also be ordered by phone or online. Here are two sources: Teaching Resource Center Catalog (1-800-833-3389) and at **www.trcabc.com**

School Specialty Beckley-Cardy (1-888-222-1332) and at **www.beckleycardy.com**

Initial *b*

> Happy **b**irthday to you,
>
> Happy **b**irthday to me,
>
> All the gifts that you give me
>
> Must **b**egin with a ***b***!
>
> So, please give me a _____,
>
> And a _____ that is green,
>
> And the very **b**est _____
>
> That you've ever seen!

MATERIALS

* 34" x 42" pocket chart
* 10 sentence strips
* colored markers
* pictures for initial *b* words (See pages 68–69.)
* drawing paper
* crayons

Getting Started

1. Write the poem above on sentence strips.

2. You may want to write each initial *b* in a second color.

3. Photocopy and color the pictures. Glue them onto cardstock and cut them out.

4. Write the following words on sentence strips, and cut into separate words:

ball	balloon	banana
bicycle	boat	book

Introducing the Poem

Place the sentence strips with the poem in the pocket chart. First, read aloud the poem to children. Then have children read the poem with you. Ask children how many blank spaces there are in the poem. (three) Explain that they will be filling each space with a picture and matching word that begin with the /b/ sound and the letter *b*.

Ask children to find all the words in the poem that begin with the letter *b* and make the /b/ sound. (*birthday* in lines 1 and 2; *begin* in line 4; *best* in line 7)

Strengthening Phonics Skills

Display the six pictures for initial *b* along the chalkboard ledge. Display the word strips in a separate row. Then ask volunteers to choose a picture, say its name, find its matching word strip, and place them in the poem.

Whenever three *b* words and pictures have been placed in the poem, ask the children to read the poem aloud with the new words. Continue until all six words have been used. Then encourage children to come up with words of their own. There are many nouns that begin with *b*, for example: *band, bear, bed, bell, bat, bank, basket, bird,* and *bugle.*

Ask children to identify the rhymes in the poem. (*me* and *b*; *green* and *seen*)

Going Beyond the Pocket Chart

Book Titles Have children make up book titles that contain two to five words. Explain that at least two of the words must begin with *b*. Their book titles may be serious or funny, for example: *Big Bear Takes a Bath.* Then have children use drawing paper and crayons to illustrate a book cover for their title. Children can write their name as author and illustrator. Display children's book covers on a bulletin board. Title the display "Our **B**est **B**ooks."

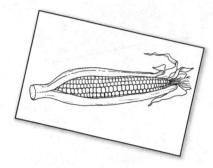

Initial c

> I'm thinking about
>
> All kinds of food.
>
> They begin with **c**.
>
> What **c**an you include?
>
> I **c**an include (a) _____.

MATERIALS

* 34" x 42" or 24" x 24" pocket chart
* 7 sentence strips
* colored markers
* pictures for initial *c* words (See pages 70–71.)
* pictures for distracter words (banana, nut, muffin, hot dog, lemon, peach)
* milk cartons or small boxes
* construction paper
* crayons
* scissors
* glue

Getting Started

1. Write the riddle above on sentence strips.

2. You may want to write each initial *c* in a second color.

3. Photocopy and color the pictures. Glue them onto cardstock and cut them out.

4. Write the following words on sentence strips, and cut into separate words:

corn	**c**arrot	**c**auliflower
cucumber	**c**ake	**c**ookie

Introducing the Riddle

Place the sentence strips with the rhyming riddle in the pocket chart. Read aloud the riddle to children. Then invite them to read it along with you. Explain that the answer to the riddle must begin with the /k/ sound and the letter *c*. Say: *Let's see how many words we can use to answer the riddle!* Then tell children that

you are going to show them two pictures of foods. They will have to choose the picture whose name begins with the /k/ sound and the letter *c*.

Strengthening Phonics Skills · · · · · · · · · · · · · · · · ✳

Place the pictures for *banana* and *corn* in the pocket chart next to the last sentence. Ask children to say the names of the pictures aloud. Ask: *Which picture has a name that begins with the /k/ sound?* (*corn*) Place the picture in the last line of the riddle. Then place the word strip for *corn* next to the picture. Ask: *What sound does the letter* c *make at the beginning of* corn? (/k/) Then ask if there are other words in the riddle that begin with the letter *c* and make the /k/ sound. (*can* in lines 4 and 5) Some children may point out that the word *kinds* in line 2 also makes the /k/ sound. Compliment them on their listening skills, and explain that *k* is another letter that makes the /k/ sound. Continue with the riddle, using the pictures for *nut* and *carrot, cauliflower* and *muffin, hot dog* and *cucumber, cake* and *lemon,* and *peach* and *cookie.* Then ask children to come up with their own food words to answer the riddle (for example: *cantaloupe, cocoa, coleslaw, cottage cheese, collard greens,* and *custard*). Finally, have them identify the rhyming words in the riddle. (*food* and *include*)

Going Beyond the Pocket Chart · · · ·

Word Cubes Place the following word strips in the pocket chart: *corn, carrots,* and *cake.* Ask children to say each word and listen for the /k/ sound. Then ask children to think of other words that begin with the /k/ sound and the letter *c,* such as *cat, cot, car, cape,* and *cut.* Write their suggestions on the chalkboard.

Explain to children that they are going to make word cubes from empty milk cartons or small boxes. Children will cut out six different colored construction-paper squares to cover each side of the container. On each square, they will write a word that begins with the letter *c* and the /k/ sound. Have children glue the paper squares on the sides of the container. Children can then roll the cube, read the word on top, and use it in a sentence.

Initial *d*

I can think of **d**elightful things

Whose names begin with this letter—

Like a **d**affodil or a **d**elicious **d**essert.

Can you think of something better?

A _____ is **d**elightful!

✿ MATERIALS ✿

* 34" x 42" or 24" x 24" pocket chart
* 7 sentence strips
* colored markers
* pictures for initial *d* words (See pages 72–73.)
* pictures for distracter words (Select pictures for other initial consonants.)

Getting Started

1. Write the riddle above on sentence strips.

2. You may want to write each initial *d* in a second color.

3. Photocopy and color the pictures. Glue them onto cardstock and cut them out.

4. Write the following words on sentence strips, and cut into separate words:

dog	**d**oll	**d**olphin
duck	**d**aisy	**d**inosaur

Introducing the Riddle

Place the sentence strips with the rhyming riddle in the pocket chart. Read aloud the riddle to children, and invite them to read it along with you. Explain that the answer to the riddle must begin with the /d/ sound and the letter *d*. Call on volunteers to identify all the words in the riddle that begin with the /d/ sound and the letter *d.* (*delightful* in line 1; *daffodil, delicious,* and *dessert* in line 3; *delightful* in line 5) Then ask: *How many different words do you think we can come up with to answer the riddle?* On the chalkboard, write two or three estimates that children suggest. Explain that at the end of the activity, it will be fun to compare the number of words they came up with to their estimates.

Strengthening Phonics Skills

Place a pile of 10 to 12 pictures near the pocket chart. The pile should contain the six initial *d* pictures, as well as pictures whose names begin with other consonants. In a separate pile, place the word strips for the initial *d* words. Call on a volunteer to take a picture from the top of the pile and say its name. If the picture's name begins with the /d/ sound, such as *dog,* the child should place the picture and its corresponding word strip in the last sentence of the riddle and read it aloud: *A dog is delightful!* If the picture's name begins with a consonant other than *d,* such as *boat,* the child should say: *A boat is not delightful!* Continue until all pictures have been selected. Then ask children to think of other words that answer the riddle (for example: *dollar, dad, dance, dawn, doe, donkey, dove, day, dinner,* and *deck*). Be sure to total the number of words they came up with and compare it with their estimates.

Finally, have children identify the rhyming words in the riddle. (*letter* and *better*)

Going Beyond the Pocket Chart

Daffy Sentences Write the following "daffy" sentences on the chalkboard. Explain that the underlined word in each sentence begins with the wrong letter. Ask children to read each daffy sentence, change the initial letter of the underlined word to the letter *d,* and then read the sentence again.

1. A <u>lime</u> equals ten pennies. (*dime*)
2. I put my sandwich on a <u>fish</u>. (*dish*)
3. Tie the boat to the <u>sock</u>. (*dock*)
4. I can <u>jig</u> with a shovel. (dig)
5. Can you <u>five</u> into the pool? (*dive*)
6. The sun comes up at <u>yawn</u>. (*dawn*)

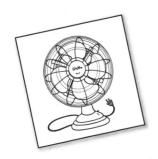

Initial *f*

Can you think of words that begin like **f**ix?

Perhaps you can think of **f**ive or six.

Or perhaps **f**ifteen or **f**orty-**f**our,

Can you possibly think of even more?

Give it a try, let's have some **f**un,

But start by thinking of only one!

Getting Started

* Write the poem above on sentence strips.
* You may want to write each initial *f* in a second color.
* Write the following words on sentence strips, and cut into separate words:

fan	farm	feather
foot	fire	fork

Introducing the Poem

Place the sentence strips with the poem in the pocket chart. Read aloud the poem to children. Then invite them to read the poem with you. Ask children to point out the words in the poem that begin with the /f/ sound and the letter *f*. (*fix* in line 1; *five* in line 2; *fifteen* and *forty-four* in line 3; *fun* in line 5)

Explain to children that first they will identify pictures whose names begin with the sound /f/ and the letter *f*. Then they will think of words on their own. Ask: *Do you think you can come up with fifteen words? Forty-four words? Let's see!*

Strengthening Phonics Skills · · · · · · · ※

Use the initial *f* pictures and distracter pictures to set up choice options that you think are appropriate for your children. For example, you may want to place one initial *f* picture and one distracter picture, or one initial *f* picture and two distracter pictures in the pocket chart. Each time children identify an initial *f* picture, ask them to find the corresponding word strip (displayed along the chalkboard ledge), and place it beside the picture. Continue until all six pictures and words have been identified. Then challenge children to come up with initial *f* words of their own (for example: *fact, fair, fall, family, far, fast, father, feed, few,* and *find*).

Finally, have children identify the rhyming words in the poem. (*fix* and *six; four* and *more, fun* and *one*)

Going Beyond the Pocket Chart

Five Fingers Have each child trace his or her hand. Then ask children to write one word that begins with the /f/ sound and the letter *f* on each finger of their traced hand. They may want to write each word in a different color. Display children's work on a bulletin board titled "**Five Fingers for** Initial *f* Words."

Initial g

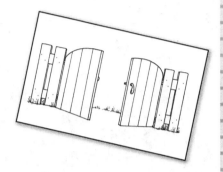

I'm thinking of a word

That begins with **g**.

It rhymes with <u>coat</u>. (rhyming replacement word)

Go find it for me!

The word is (**g**<u>oat</u>).

❖ MATERIALS ❖

✳ 34" x 42" or 24" x 24" pocket chart

✳ 9 sentence strips

✳ colored markers

✳ pictures for initial *g* words (See pages 76–77.)

✳ craft paper

✳ crayons or paints

Getting Started

1. Write the riddle above on sentence strips.

2. You may want to write each initial *g* in a second color.

3. Photocopy and color the pictures. Glue them onto cardstock and cut them out.

4. Write the following words on sentence strips, and cut into separate words:

goat	game	gate
goose	gift	girl

Rhyming Replacement Words

The following are the rhyming replacement words to be used in line 3 of the riddle. Write them on sentence strips and cut into separate words:

coat (for *goat*), name (for *game*), late (for *gate*), moose (for *goose*), lift (for *gift*), whirl (for *girl*)

Introducing the Riddle

Place the word strips for the *g* words in one pile and their corresponding pictures in a second pile. Then place the sentence strips with the first rhyming riddle in the pocket chart. Read aloud the riddle to children, and ask them to read it along with you. Explain that the answer to the riddle has to rhyme with the word *coat* and begin with the /g/ sound and the letter *g*.

Strengthening Phonics Skills

After children have figured out the answer (*goat*) ask a volunteer to find the word strip and the picture for *goat* in each pile. Have the child place the word strip and picture in the answer space and read the sentence aloud: *The word is* goat. Then continue to use the riddle by placing a new rhyming replacement word in line 3, and asking children to figure out the new rhyming answer that begins with the /g/ sound and the letter *g*. Repeat until all six words have been used. Then ask children if they can find any other words in the riddle that begin with the /g/ sound and the letter *g*. (*Go* in line 4)

Encourage children to make up some riddles of their own by thinking of a word that begins with *g* and supplying a rhyming word for line 3 of the poem. Here are some examples: *so* for *go; not* for *got; stood* for *good; sold* for *gold; save* for *gave; rather* for *gather;* and *rain* for *gain.*

Going Beyond the Pocket Chart

A Garden of Words Cover a bulletin board with a sheet of craft paper. The title of the bulletin board can be "A **G**arden of Words That Begin With *g*." Invite each child to draw or paint a picture of something that grows in a garden, such as a flower, tree, or bush. What makes this garden special is that each plant should have a word written on it that begins with the letter *g*. Encourage children to make their plants interesting and colorful, and help each child choose a different word to write on his or her creation.

Initial *h*

> I **h**ave a **h**at.
>
> She **h**as a **h**oe.
>
> **H**e **h**as a **h**orn.
>
> It's your turn to go!
>
> I **h**ave a _____.

❄ MATERIALS ❄

* 34" x 42" or 24" x 24" pocket chart
* 7 sentence strips
* colored markers
* pictures for initial *h* words (See pages 78–79.)
* pictures for distracter words (Select pictures for other initial consonants.)
* crayons
* drawing paper

Getting Started

1. Write the riddle above on sentence strips.

2. You may want to write each initial *h* in a second color.

3. Photocopy and color the pictures. Glue them onto cardstock and cut them out.

4. Write the following words on sentence strips, and cut into separate words:

helmet	**h**at	**h**ot dog
horse	**h**ammer	**h**ouse

Introducing the Riddle

Place the sentence strips with the rhyming riddle in the pocket chart. Read aloud the riddle to children. Then invite them to read it along with you. Explain that the answer to the riddle must begin with the /h/ sound and the letter *h*. Say: *Let's see how many different words we can use to answer the riddle!* Then tell children that you are going to show them a group of pictures. They will have to choose a picture whose name begins with the /h/ sound and the letter *h*.

Strengthening Phonics Skills

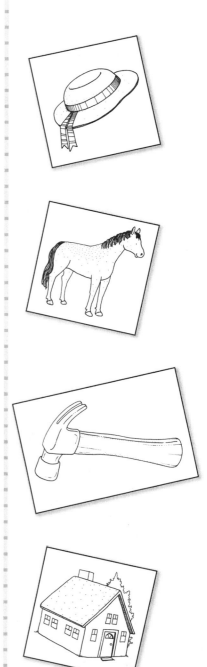

Place a group of four pictures beside or under the last sentence. Use two initial *h* pictures and two distracter pictures. Explain to children that two pictures have names that begin with the /h/ sound and two pictures do not. Have children say the names of the pictures aloud. Then call on a volunteer to identify one of the pictures whose name begins with the /h/ sound to answer the riddle. After a picture is identified, have the child place it in the last sentence of the riddle. Then have the child place the corresponding word strip beside the picture and read aloud the sentence. Call on another volunteer to find the other /h/ picture in the group, and follow the same procedure. Continue forming picture groups until all the pictures that begin with the /h/ sound have been used to answer the riddle. Then ask children to find other words in the riddle that begin with the letter *h* and make the /h/ sound. (*have* and *hat* in line 1; *has* and *hoe* in line 2; *He, has,* and *horn* in line 3; *have* in line 5)

Give children an opportunity to come up with their own words to answer the riddle (for example: *hamburger, head, hand, helicopter, hippopotamus, hood,* and *hook*). Finally, ask children to identify the rhyming words in the riddle. (*hoe* and *go*)

Going Beyond the Pocket Chart

"How Many" Questions Write a variety of "how many" questions, such as the following, on the chalkboard:

> **H**ow many fingers do you **h**ave?
> **H**ow many teeth do you **h**ave?
> **H**ow many pets do you **h**ave?

Call on children to read and answer the questions. Then have them choose one of the questions, write a sentence that answers it, and draw a picture to illustrate their answer.

Initial *j*

> **J**ack likes cherry **j**am.
>
> **J**ill likes it too.
>
> **J**enny likes apple **j**am,
>
> So does **J**ane and so does Sam.
>
> But there are other things to like,
>
> Let's name a few today.
>
> There's **j**ust one thing to keep in mind,
>
> They must begin with **j**!

MATERIALS

* 42" x 58" pocket chart or two smaller pocket charts
* 10 sentence strips
* colored markers
* pictures for initial *j* words (See pages 80–81.)
* pictures for distracter words (Select pictures for other initial consonants.)
* drawing paper
* crayons

Getting Started

1. Write the poem above on sentence strips.

2. You may want to write each initial *j* in a second color.

3. Photocopy and color the pictures. Glue them onto cardstock and cut them out.

4. Write the following words on sentence strips, and cut into separate words:

jaguar	jacket	jack-o-lantern
jeans	jet	juggler

Introducing the Poem

Place the sentence strips with the poem in the pocket chart. Read aloud the poem to children. Then ask children to read the poem along with you. Call on several volunteers to identify the words in the poem that begin with the /j/ sound and the letter *j*. (*Jack* and *jam* in line 1; *Jill* in line 2; *Jenny* and *jam* in line 3; *Jane* in line 4; *just* in line 7)

Explain to children that you are going to show them two pictures at a time. They will have to identify the picture whose name begins with the /j/ sound and the letter *j*. Then say: *Let's see how many things we can name that begin with the /j/ sound made by the letter* j.

Strengthening Phonics Skills

Place one initial *j* picture and one distracter picture under the poem. Call on a volunteer to say each picture name aloud, and then identify the picture whose name begins with the /j/ sound. Remove the distracter picture and ask another volunteer to find the matching word strip and place it next to the picture. (The word strips for the initial *j* words can be displayed in another part of the pocket chart.) Continue until all six initial *j* pictures and words have been identified. Then ask children to think of other things they like that begin with the /j/ sound and the letter *j* (for example: *jogging, joke, joy, juice, jumping, jungle, journal, jewelry, June, July,* and *January*).

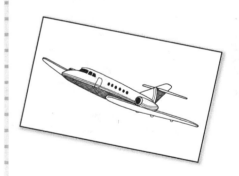

Finally, have children identify the rhymes in the poem. (*jam* and *Sam; today* and *j*)

Going Beyond the Pocket Chart

January and June Ask children to write the headings *January* and *June* on a sheet of paper. Under each month's name, have children list the kinds of activities they like to do in that month. Then invite children to draw a picture of their favorite activity and write a sentence or two about it. Have them complete one of the following sentence frames: "I like to _____ in January" or "I like to _____ in June."

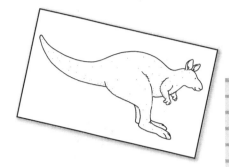

Initial *k*

Kelly called to Katy,

"Will you come out and play?

We'll fly our kites and ride our bikes,

It's such a pretty day!"

Then Katy said to Kelly,

"I can't come out to play,

Unless I hear you say a word

That begins with the letter *k*!"

✺ MATERIALS ✺

✳ 42" x 58" pocket chart or two smaller pocket charts

✳ 10 sentence strips

✳ colored markers

✳ pictures for initial *k* words (See pages 82–83.)

✳ pictures for distracter words (Select pictures for other initial consonants.)

✳ crayons or paints

✳ drawing paper

Getting Started ················· ✳

✳ Write the poem above on sentence strips.

✳ You may want to write each initial *k* in a second color.

✳ Write the following words on sentence strips, and cut into separate words:

koala	king	kangaroo
key	kettle	kiss

Introducing the Poem ·············· ✳

Place the sentence strips with the poem in the pocket chart, and read aloud the poem to children. Then invite children to read the poem along with you. Ask volunteers to find all the words in the poem that begin with the letter *k* and make the /k/ sound. (*Kelly* and *Katy* in line 1; *kites* in line 3; *Katy* and *Kelly* in line 5) If children point out that the words *called*, *come*, and *can't* also begin with the /k/ sound, compliment them on their listening skills and explain that the letters *k* and *c* both make the /k/ sound.

Explain that in the activity they will do today, they will add pictures and words to the pocket chart whose names begin with the letter *k* and the /k/ sound.

Strengthening Phonics Skills

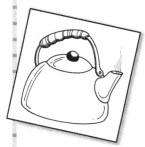

Ask 10 children to come to the front of the room, and give each child a picture. Six children should have pictures for initial *k* words. The rest should have pictures whose names begin with other consonants. Have each child, in turn, say the name of his or her picture. If a child has a picture whose name begins with the /k/ sound and the letter *k*, such as *king*, the child places the picture in the pocket chart. If a child has a picture whose name begins with another consonant, such as *wagon*, the child puts the picture aside. After each child has had a turn, display the initial *k* words on word strips. Call on volunteers to place the word strips next to their corresponding pictures. Then ask children to think of other initial *k* words on their own (for example: *karate, keep, kind, kid, kindergarten, kitten, kennel, kayak, kickball,* and *kite*).

Finally, have children identify the rhymes in the poem. (*play* and *day*; *play* and *k*)

Going Beyond the Pocket Chart

Animal Kingdom Write the following animals' names on the chalkboard: *kangaroo, koala, katydid, kookaburra, kiwi,* and *Komodo dragon.* If possible, have library books or other resources available that contain pictures of the animals.

Ask children to select one animal and write a few sentences about it, describing what it looks like, where it lives, or what it eats. Then invite children to draw or paint a picture of the animal. Display children's work on a bulletin board with the title "Our Animal **K**ingdom for Initial *k*."

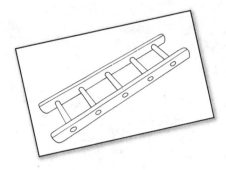

Initial *l*

There are **l**ots of words

That begin with **l**

That I can read

And I can spell,

Like _____ and _____,

And **l**ightning too,

And **l**ollipops for me and you!

MATERIALS

* 34" x 42" pocket chart
* 9 sentence strips
* colored markers
* pictures for initial *l* words (See pages 84–85.)
* drawing paper
* crayons

Getting Started

1. Write the poem above on sentence strips.

2. You may want to write each initial *l* in a second color.

3. Photocopy and color the pictures. Glue them onto cardstock and cut them out.

4. Write the following words on sentence strips, and cut into separate words:

lion	lemon	ladder
lamp	lamb	ladybug

Introducing the Poem

Place the sentence strips with the poem in the pocket chart. Read aloud the poem to children. Then have

children read the poem along with you. Point out the two blank spaces, and explain to children that they need to fill each space with a picture and matching word that begin with the /l/ sound and the letter *l*.

Ask children to find other words in the poem that begin with the letter *l* and make the /l/ sound. (*lots* in line 1; *like* in line 5; *lightning* in line 6; *lollipops* in line 7)

Strengthening Phonics Skills

Display the six pictures for initial *l* along the chalkboard ledge. Display the word strips for the pictures in a separate row. Then ask volunteers to choose a picture, say its name, find its matching word strip, and place them in the poem.

Each time two *l* words have been placed in the poem, have children read the poem aloud with the new words. Continue until all the *l* words and pictures have been used. Then encourage children to come up with words of their own (for example: *lily, leaf, letter, lizard, lake, land, leg, library, light,* and *log*). Finally, have children identify the rhymes in the poem. (*l* and *spell; too* and *you*)

Going Beyond the Pocket Chart

Lots of Questions Ask children to write and illustrate a question in which at least two of the words begin with the letter *l*. Tell them to make their questions as silly or as funny as they like. Here are several examples to use as models: Can a **l**ion **l**eap? Can a **l**izard **l**augh? Do **l**adybugs **l**ike to **l**earn? Can a **l**amb climb a **l**adder? Display the pictures and word strips for initial *l* so children can refer to them, but explain that they may use any word that begins with *l*. Encourage them to use a picture dictionary. Create a bulletin board for children's questions and illustrations and title it "**L**ots of Questions to **L**augh About!"

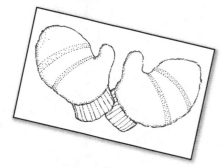

Initial *m*

Movies, museums, and a merry-go-round,

Music that makes the most wonderful sound.

Maples in meadows and mountains so high,

Macaroni and mangos you might want to try.

Messages and mail from friends far and near,

Mornings in May when the sky is so clear.

How many marvelous things can you name?

Join in and play the initial *m* game!

❂ MATERIALS ❂

✳ 42" x 58" pocket chart or two smaller pocket charts

✳ 10 sentence strips

✳ colored markers

✳ pictures for initial *m* words (See pages 86–87.)

✳ pictures for distracter words (Select pictures for other initial consonants.)

✳ audiocassette of lively music

✳ index cards

Getting Started

1. Write the poem above on sentence strips.

2. You may want to write each initial *m* in a second color.

3. Photocopy and color the pictures. Glue them onto cardstock and cut them out.

4. Write the following words on sentence strips, and cut into separate words:

magnet	moon	mask
monkey	mittens	muffin

Introducing the Poem

Place the sentence strips with the poem in the pocket chart. Read aloud the poem to children, then invite them to read it along with you. You may want children to form two groups, with each group reciting alternate lines of the poem. Then call on volunteers to identify all the words that begin with the /m/ sound and the letter *m*. (*movies, museums,* and *merry-go-round* in line 1; *music, makes,* and *most* in line 2; *maples, meadows,* and *mountains* in line 3; *macaroni, mangos,* and *might* in line 4; *messages* and *mail* in line 5; *mornings* and *May* in line 6; *many* and *marvelous* in line 7) Then say: *Let's see how many other things we can name that begin with the /m/ sound and the letter* m.

Strengthening Phonics Skills

Place a pile of 10 to 12 pictures near the pocket chart. The pile should contain the pictures whose names begin with *m* mixed in with pictures whose names begin with other consonants. In a second pile, place the word strips for the *m* words. Call on a volunteer to take a picture from the top of the pile and say its name. If the picture's name begins with the /m/ sound, such as *magnet,* the child should place the picture and its corresponding word strip in the pocket chart. If the picture's name begins with a consonant other than *m,* such as *corn,* the child should put it aside. Continue until all pictures have been selected.

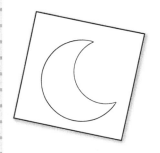

Next, challenge children to think of their own words that begin with the /m/ sound (for example: *menu, milk, marshmallow, mom, minute,* and *me*). You may want to play some lively music, and as each child names a word, he or she gets up and marches around the room, until all the children are marching. Be sure to help any child who has difficulty by offering a word clue, for example: *This is something good to drink.* (*milk*) Finally, have children identify the rhyming words in the poem. (*merry-go-round* and *sound; high* and *try; near* and *clear; name* and *game*)

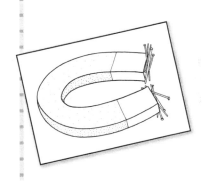

Going Beyond the Pocket Chart

Matching Word Game Have pairs of children make two word cards each for at least eight words that begin with *m.* Have them mix up the cards and place them facedown. The first player turns over two cards and reads the words. If the words match, the player keeps them. If they don't match, the player turns them facedown. Children play until all the word pairs are taken. The player with the most pairs wins.

Initial *n*

Many words begin with **n**.

Can you **n**ame **n**ine or ten?

Let's start off with *n*ice and *n*ew.

This will **n**ot be hard to do!

The word _____ begins with **n**.

○ MATERIALS ○

* ❋ 34" x 42" or 24" x 24" pocket chart
* ❋ 7 sentence strips
* ❋ colored markers
* ❋ pictures for initial *n* words (See pages 88–89.)
* ❋ pictures for distracter words (Select pictures for other initial consonants.)
* ❋ crayons
* ❋ drawing paper

Getting Started ·········· ❋

1. Write the riddle above on sentence strips.

2. You may want to write each initial *n* in a second color.

3. Photocopy and color the pictures. Glue them onto cardstock and cut them out.

4. Write the following words on sentence strips, and cut into separate words:

nut	**n**ecklace	**n**urse
newspaper	**n**eedle	**n**est

Introducing the Riddle ········ ❋

Place the sentence strips with the rhyming riddle in the pocket chart. Read aloud the riddle to children, and invite them to read it along with you. Ask children to point out the words in the riddle that begin with the /n/ sound and the letter *n*. (*name* and *nine* in line 2; *nice* and *new* in line 3; *not* in line 4)

Explain to children that first they will identify pictures whose names begin with the sound /n/ and the letter *n*. Then they will think of words on their own. Ask: *Do you think you can come up with more than nine or ten words? Let's see!*

Strengthening Phonics Skills

Use the initial *n* pictures and distracter pictures to set up choice options that you think are appropriate for your children. For example, you may want to use one initial *n* picture and one distracter picture, or one initial *n* picture and two distracter pictures. Each time children identify an initial *n* picture, have them place it in the last sentence of the riddle. Then ask them to find the corresponding word strip (displayed along the chalkboard ledge), place it beside the picture, and read aloud the sentence. Continue until all six pictures and words have been identified. Then challenge children to come up with initial *n* words of their own (for example: *note, nap, nature, near, neat, need, neighbor, never, next,* and *night*).

Finally, have children identify the rhymes in the poem. (*n* and *ten; new* and *do*)

Going Beyond the Pocket Chart

Nice Things Use the following question as a heading for a bulletin board: "What is **n**ice?" Ask children to respond to the question by writing a sentence or two about something or someone that they think is nice. Invite them to illustrate their sentences.

Initial *p*

Mom bought me a **p**et,

It comes when I call,

Its name begins with *p*,

My **p**et is best of all!

My **p**et is a _____.

Getting Started

1. Write the riddle above on sentence strips.

2. You may want to write each initial *p* in a second color.

3. Photocopy and color the pictures. Glue them onto cardstock and cut them out.

4. Write the following words on sentence strips, and cut into separate words:

puppy	**p**arakeet	**p**ony
panda	**p**enguin	**p**ig

Introducing the Riddle

Place the sentence strips with the rhyming riddle in the pocket chart. Read aloud the riddle to children. Then ask children to read it along with you. Explain that the answer to the riddle should begin with the /p/ sound and the letter *p*. Ask: *Do you think there can be more than one answer to the riddle?* Then tell children

that you are going to show them two pictures of animals. Have them choose the picture whose name begins with the /p/ sound and the letter *p*.

Strengthening Phonics Skills

Place the pictures for *rabbit* and *puppy* in the pocket chart next to the last sentence. Ask children to say aloud the names of the pictures. Ask: *Which picture has a name that begins with the /p/ sound?* (*puppy*) Place the picture of the puppy in the last line of the riddle. Then place the word strip for *puppy* next to the picture. Ask children what sound the letter *p* makes at the beginning of the word *puppy*. (/p/) Then ask if there are any other words in the riddle that begin with the letter *p* and make the /p/ sound. (*pet* in lines 1, 4, and 5) Follow the same procedure using the pictures for *goat* and *parakeet*; *duck* and *pony*; *horse* and *panda*; *monkey* and *penguin*; and *lamb* and *pig*. Finally, ask children to identify the rhyming words in the riddle. (*call* and *all*)

Going Beyond the Pocket Chart

Puzzles Place the following pictures in the pocket chart: *puppy, parakeet, pony, panda, penguin,* and *pig*. Ask children to say each word and listen for the /p/ sound. Display the word strips for the pictures, and call on volunteers to place the word next to its picture.

Explain to children that they are going to make initial *p* puzzles using the pictures and words in the pocket chart. Cut several large pieces of tagboard into six to eight puzzle-shaped pieces. Make copies of the pictures for initial *p*. Have children work in small groups, choose a picture to glue on each puzzle piece, and then write the word on the same puzzle piece. Have each group put their initial *p* puzzles together. Keep the puzzles in your reading/language arts learning center so that children may use them frequently to reinforce initial *p*.

Initial *qu*

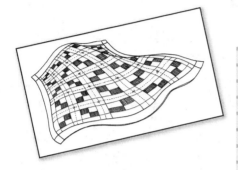

I'm thinking of a word

That begins with **qu**.

It rhymes with <u>seen</u>. (rhyming replacement word)

Do you know it too?

The word is (**qu**een).

Getting Started

1. Write the riddle above on sentence strips.

2. You may want to write each initial *qu* in a second color.

3. Photocopy and color the pictures. Glue them onto cardstock and cut them out.

4. Write the following words on sentence strips, and cut into separate words:

queen	**qu**ail	**qu**ilt
quill	**qu**iet	**qu**arter

Rhyming Replacement Words

The following are the rhyming replacement words to be used in line 3 of the riddle. Write them on sentence strips and cut into separate words:

seen (for *queen*), mail (for *quail*), tilt (for *quilt*), fill (for *quill*), diet (for *quiet*), shorter (for *quarter*)

MATERIALS

* 34" x 42" or 24" x 24" pocket chart
* 8 sentence strips
* colored markers
* pictures for initial *qu* words (See pages 92–93.)
* pencils
* paper

Introducing the Riddle

Place the pictures for the *qu* words in one pile and their corresponding word strips in another pile. Then place the sentence strips with the first rhyming riddle in the pocket chart. Read the riddle to children, and ask them to read it along with you. Explain that the answer to the riddle has to rhyme with the word *seen* and begin with the /kw/ sound and the letters *qu*.

Strengthening Phonics Skills

After children have figured out the answer (*queen*), ask a volunteer to find the picture and the word strip for *queen* in each pile. Have the child place the picture and word strip in the answer space and read aloud the sentence: *The word is* queen. Then continue to use the riddle by placing a new rhyming replacement word in line 3, and asking children to figure out the new rhyming answer that begins with the /kw/ sound and the letters *qu*. Repeat until all words have been used.

Encourage children to make up some riddles of their own by thinking of a word that begins with the letters *qu* and then supplying a rhyming word for line 3 of the poem. Here are some examples: *sick* for *quick*; *fit* for *quit*; *kite* for *quite*; *pack* for *quack*; *fizz* for *quiz*; and *bake* for *quake*.

Going Beyond the Pocket Chart

Questions Ask children to write a question that uses one of the following words: *quiet(ly)*, *quick(ly)*, *quack*, *quilt*, or *quarter*. Their question may be serious or silly. Then have pairs of children exchange papers and write answers to each other's questions. Give children the opportunity to share their questions and answers by reading them aloud. You may also want to display children's work on a bulletin board titled "**Qu**estions and Answers."

Initial r

You don't have to look very far

To find words that begin with an **r**.

Like a **r**ock and a **r**iver outside,

Like a **r**oad where we take a long **r**ide.

Like a _____ and a _____ and a **r**ing,

Like a **r**obin that comes in the spring.

◎ MATERIALS ◎

❋ 34" x 42" pocket chart

❋ 8 sentence strips

❋ colored markers

❋ pictures for initial *r* words (See pages 94–95.)

❋ pictures for distracter words (Select pictures for other initial consonants.)

❋ pencils

❋ paper

Getting Started

1. Write the poem above on sentence strips.

2. You may want to write each initial *r* in a second color.

3. Photocopy and color the pictures. Glue them onto cardstock and cut them out.

4. Write the following words on sentence strips, and cut into separate words:

rabbit	rose	rake
rocket	rainbow	robot

Introducing the Poem

Place the sentence strips with the poem in the pocket chart, and read aloud the poem to children. Then invite them to read the poem with you. Ask children how many blank spaces they see in the poem. (two)

Explain that they will be filling each space with a picture and matching word that begin with the /r/ sound that is made by the letter *r*.

Ask children to find all the words in the poem that begin with the /r/ sound and the letter *r*. (*rock* and *river* in line 3; *road* and *ride* in line 4; *ring* in line 5; *robin* in line 6)

Strengthening Phonics Skills ·········※

Use the initial *r* pictures and distracter pictures to set up choice options that you think are appropriate for your children. You may want to use one initial *r* picture and one distracter picture, or one initial *r* picture and two distracter pictures. Whenever children place an initial *r* picture in the poem, have them find the corresponding word strip (displayed on the chalkboard ledge), and place it beside the picture. Each time children complete the poem with two initial *r* pictures and words, invite them to read aloud the poem. Continue until all six words have been used to complete the poem. Then encourage children to come up with words of their own (for example: *rectangle, race, ruler, raisin, run, read, real, red, remember,* and *rug*).

Finally, have children identify the rhymes in the poem. (*far* and *r*; *outside* and *ride; ring* and *spring*)

Going Beyond the Pocket Chart

What to Read Ask children to write a few sentences that describe the kinds of things they like to read about, and then give the title of a favorite book. Invite children to read aloud their sentences to the class, and tell whether their favorite book title contains any words that begin with the letter *r*. Display children's writing on a bulletin board with the heading "We Like to **R**ead!"

Initial s

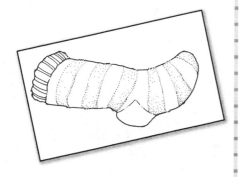

I'm thinking of a word.

It begins with an **s**.

It rhymes with _meal_. (rhyming replacement word)

See if you can guess!

The word is (**s**_eal_).

Getting Started

1. Write the riddle above on sentence strips.

2. You may want to write each initial *s* in a second color.

3. Photocopy and color the pictures. Glue them onto cardstock and cut them out.

4. Write the following words on sentence strips, and cut into separate words:

seal	sack	sun
saddle	sink	sock

Rhyming Replacement Words

The following are the rhyming replacement words to be used in line 3 of the riddle. Write them on sentence strips and cut into separate words:

meal (for *seal*), back (for *sack*), fun (for *sun*), paddle (for *saddle*), pink (for *sink*), rock (for *sock*)

MATERIALS

* 34" x 42" or 24" x 24" pocket chart
* 15 sentence strips
* colored markers
* pictures for initial *s* words (See pages 96–97.)
* drawing paper
* crayons

Introducing the Riddle

Place the word strips for the *s* words in one pile and their corresponding pictures in another pile. Then place the sentence strips with the rhyming riddle in the pocket chart. Read the first riddle to children, and ask them to read it along with you. Explain that the answer to the riddle has to rhyme with the word *meal* and begin with the /s/ sound and the letter *s*.

Strengthening Phonics Skills

After children have figured out the answer (*seal*) ask a volunteer to find the picture and the word strip for *seal* in each pile. Have the child place the picture and word strip in the answer space and read aloud the sentence: *The word is* seal. Then continue to use the riddle by placing a new rhyming replacement word in line 3, and asking children to figure out the new rhyming answer that begins with the /s/ sound and the letter *s*. Repeat until all six words have been used. Then ask children if there are any other words in the riddle that begin with the /s/ sound and the letter *s*. (*See* in line 4)

Encourage children to make up some riddles of their own by thinking of a word that begins with *s* and supplying a rhyming word for line 3 of the poem. Here are some examples: *pail* for *sail* or *sale*; *band* for *sand*; *me* for *sea* or *see*; *feed* for *seed*; *kick* for *sick*; *dad* for *sad*; *paw* for *saw*; and *king* for *sing*.

Going Beyond the Pocket Chart

A Song Write the following familiar song on sentence strips and place it in the pocket chart:

> A **s**ailor went to **s**ea, **s**ea, **s**ea
> To **s**ee what he could **s**ee, **s**ee, **s**ee.
> But all that he could **s**ee, **s**ee, **s**ee
> Was the bottom of the deep blue **s**ea, **s**ea, **s**ea!

Recite the verse with children, and ask them to identify the words that begin with *s* and make the /s/ sound. Be sure to point out that *sea* means "a body of water," and *see* means "look at." Then have children substitute other *s* words in the song for "a sailor," such as, *a salmon, a salamander, Susan,* and *six singers.* Finally, have children draw a picture to illustrate one of the versions and label their picture with the appropriate sentence (for example, "Six seals went to sea").

Initial *t*

Lots of words begin with **t**.

Toy and **t**oast and **t**ag are three.

Can you name at least one more?

That would mean we now have four!

The word _____ begins with **t**.

MATERIALS

* 34" x 42" or 24" x 24" pocket chart
* 7 sentence strips
* colored markers
* pictures for initial *t* words (See pages 98–99.)
* pictures for distracter words (Select pictures for other initial consonants.)
* pencils
* paper

Getting Started

1. Write the riddle above on sentence strips.

2. You may want to write each initial *t* in a second color.

3. Photocopy and color the pictures. Glue them onto cardstock and cut them out.

4. Write the following words on sentence strips, and cut into separate words:

table	tooth	tent
tiger	tie	turkey

Introducing the Riddle

Place the sentence strips with the rhyming riddle in the pocket chart. Read aloud the riddle to children, and invite them to read it along with you. Explain that the answer to the riddle must be a word that begins with the /t/ sound and the letter *t*. Call on volunteers to identify the words in the riddle that begin with the

/t/ sound and the letter *t*. (*toy*, *toast*, and *tag* in line 2) Then ask: *How many words do you think we can come up with to answer the riddle? Do you think we can name more than ten?* Write several estimates that children suggest on the chalkboard. Explain that at the end of the activity, it will be fun to compare the number of *t* words they came up with to their estimates.

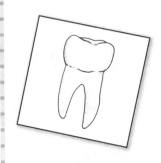

Strengthening Phonics Skills

Place a pile of 10 to 12 pictures near the pocket chart. The pile should contain the pictures whose names begin with *t* mixed in with pictures whose names begin with other consonants. In a separate pile, place the word strips for the *t* words. Call on a volunteer to take a picture from the top of the pile and say its name. If the picture's name begins with the /t/ sound, such as *table*, the child should place the picture and word strip in the last sentence of the riddle and read aloud the sentence: *The word* table *begins with* t. If the picture's name begins with a consonant other than *t*, the child should put the picture aside. Continue until all pictures have been selected. Then ask children to think of their own words to answer the riddle (for example: *turtle, taco, talk, taste, teach, team, telephone, tall,* and *test*). Be sure to total the number of words they came up with and compare it with their estimates.

Finally, have children identify the rhymes in the riddle. (*t* and *three*; *more* and *four*)

Going Beyond the Pocket Chart

Tick-Tack-Toe Invite children to play tick-tack-toe with a partner. In this game, partners will take turns writing words in a tick-tack-toe grid. One player will write words that begin with *t*, and the other player will write words that begin with another familiar consonant. Have children say each word as they write it. The first player to get a line of words wins.

For an easier variation of the game, partners can take turns saying a word and writing just the initial consonant in the grid. The first player to get a line of letters is the winner.

Initial v

V is for **v**egetables

And **v**iolets that grow.

V is for **v**oices

That sing sweet and low.

V is for **v**acations

And **v**isits to the shore.

V is for **v**anilla!

What else is **v** for?

❋ MATERIALS ❋

* ❋ 42" x 58" pocket chart or two smaller pocket charts
* ❋ 10 sentence strips
* ❋ colored markers
* ❋ pictures for initial *v* words (See pages 100–101.)
* ❋ pictures for distracter words (Select pictures for other initial consonants.)
* ❋ craft paper
* ❋ crayons or paints

Getting Started .... ❋

1. Write the poem above on sentence strips.

2. You may want to write each initial *v* in a second color.

3. Photocopy and color the pictures. Glue them onto cardstock and cut them out.

4. Write the following words on sentence strips, and cut into separate words:

vase	vet	van
valentine	vest	violin

Introducing the Poem .... ❋

Place the sentence strips with the poem in the pocket chart. Read aloud the poem to children. Then ask children to read the poem along with you. Call on several volunteers to identify all the words in the poem that begin with the /v/ sound and the letter *v*. (*vegetables* in line 1; *violets* in line 2; *voices* in line 3; *vacations* in line 5; *visits* in line 6; *vanilla* in line 7)

Explain to children that you are going to show them two pictures at a time. They will identify the picture whose name begins with the /v/ sound and the letter *v*. Then say: *Let's see how many words we can name that begin with the /v/ sound made by the letter* v.

Strengthening Phonics Skills

Place one initial *v* picture and one distracter picture under the poem. Call on a volunteer to say aloud each picture name, and then identify the picture whose name begins with the /v/ sound. Remove the distracter picture and ask another volunteer to find the matching word strip and place it next to the picture. (The word strips for the initial *v* words can be displayed in another part of the pocket chart.) Continue until all six initial *v* pictures and words have been identified. Then ask children to come up with other words on their own (for example: *very, video, village, vine, vowel, volleyball, valley, vote, view,* and *volcano*).

Finally, have children identify the rhyming words in the poem. (*grow* and *low, shore* and *for*)

Going Beyond the Pocket Chart

A Village Cover a bulletin board with a sheet of craft paper. The title of the bulletin board can be "Visit Our **V**illage." Then invite children to create a village that is filled with places and objects whose names begin with *v*. For example, the village might have a vegetable garden, a video store, a volleyball court, a veternarian's office, vines, vans, and a place for people to vote. Each object should be labeled. Encourage children to come up with creative names for buildings and stores, such as Valley View School or Vicki's Violin Shop.

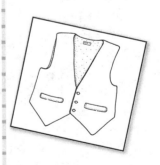

Initial *w*

Here's a game for us to play,

As **we** **w**ork in school today.

The only **w**ords that **we** can say

Should start **with** **w**, like **w**alk and **w**ay.

So if you have a **w** **w**ord,

Say it clearly so you are heard.

Stand up and say to one and all:

I can add _____ to our **W**ord **W**all!

MATERIALS

* 34" x 42" or 24" x 24" pocket chart
* 10 sentence strips
* colored markers
* pictures for initial *w* words (See pages 102–103.)
* pictures for distracter words (Select pictures for other initial consonants.)
* Word Wall
* crayons
* drawing paper

Getting Started

1. Write the poem above on sentence strips.

2. You may want to write each initial *w* in a second color.

3. Photocopy and color the pictures. Glue them onto cardstock and cut them out.

4. Write the following words on sentence strips, and cut into separate words:

wagon	well	wave
walrus	window	wig

Introducing the Poem

Place the sentence strips with the poem in the pocket chart, and read aloud the poem to children. Then invite children to read the poem along with you. Ask volunteers to find all the words in the poem that begin with the letter *w* and make the /w/ sound. (*we* and *work* in line 2; *words* and *we* in line 3; *with, walk,* and *way* in line 4; *word* in line 5; *word* and *wall* in line 8)

Explain that in the activity they will do today, they will add pictures and words to the Word Wall whose names begin with the letter *w* and the /w/ sound.

Strengthening Phonics Skills

Give 10 children pictures. Six children should have pictures for initial *w* words. The rest should have pictures whose names begin with other consonants. Have each child, in turn, say the name of his or her picture. If a child has a picture whose name begins with the /w/ sound and the letter *w*, such as *wagon,* the child says: *I can add* wagon *to our Word Wall,* and posts the picture on the Word Wall. If a child has a picture whose name begins with another consonant, such as *lion,* the child says: *I can't add* lion *to our Word Wall.* After each child has had a turn, display the initial *w* words on word strips. Call on volunteers to place the word strips next to their corresponding pictures. Then ask children to think of other initial *w* words to add to the Word Wall (for example: *wake, we, winter, water, wet,* and *win*).

Finally, have children identify the rhyming words in the poem. (*play* and *today*; *say* and *way*; *word* and *heard*; *all* and *wall*)

Going Beyond the Pocket Chart

A Fuzzy Wuzzy Tongue Twister Write the following tongue twister on chart paper:

> Fuzzy **W**uzzy was a bear.
> Fuzzy **W**uzzy had no hair.
> Fuzzy **W**uzzy wasn't fuzzy.
> **W**as he?

Recite the tongue twister several times with children. Then ask volunteers to find all the words that begin with *w,* say them aloud, and circle them.

Distribute drawing paper and crayons to children. Invite them to create a picture of Fuzzy Wuzzy and write a sentence about him. They may use a sentence from the tongue twister or make up one of their own.

Final x

> There aren't many words
>
> That end with an **x**,
>
> Like fi**x** and _____,
>
> And a name like Re**x**.
>
> If you can think of another one,
>
> Then this poem would be more fun!

MATERIALS

* 34" x 42" or 24" x 24" pocket chart
* 8 sentence strips
* colored markers
* pictures for final *x* words (See pages 104–105.)
* pictures for distracter words (Select pictures that end with other consonants.)
* crayons
* drawing paper

Getting Started

1. Write the poem above on sentence strips.

2. You may want to write each final *x* in a second color.

3. Photocopy and color the pictures. Glue them onto cardstock and cut them out.

4. Write the following words on sentence strips, and cut into separate words:

six	wax	fox
ax	box	ox

Introducing the Poem

Place the sentence strips with the poem in the pocket chart, and read aloud the poem to children. Then invite children to read the poem with you. Ask children how many blank spaces they see in the poem. (one) Explain that they will be filling that space with a picture and matching word that end with the /ks/ sound, which is made by the letter *x*.

Ask children to find the words in the poem that end with the /ks/ sound and the letter *x*. (*fix* in line 3; *Rex* in line 4)

Strengthening Phonics Skills

Use the final *x* pictures and distracter pictures to set up appropriate choice options for your children. You may want to use one final *x* picture and one distracter picture, or one final *x* picture and two distracter pictures. Whenever children place a final *x* picture in the poem, have them find the corresponding word strip (displayed on the chalkboard ledge), and place it next to the picture. When children complete the poem with a final *x* picture and word, invite them to read the poem aloud. Continue until all six words have been used to complete the poem. Then challenge children to come up with final *x* words of their own (for example: *fax, tax, Max, mix, relax, lox, lax, flax,* and *prefix*).

Finally, have children identify the rhymes in the poem. (*x* and *Rex; one* and *fun*)

Going Beyond the Pocket Chart

Ways to Relax Discuss with children the different things people do to relax or have a good time, such as reading a book, going fishing, taking a hike, or playing a game. Then ask children to write a few sentences that describe what they like to do to relax. Have them also draw a picture that shows their relaxing activity. Display children's work on a bulletin board with the heading "This is the Way We Relax."

Initial *y* and *z*

There aren't many words **y**ou see

That start with letters **y** and **z**.

There's **z**oom for **z** and **y**ell for **y**.

Take **y**our turn and give it a try!

✿ MATERIALS ✿

* 34" x 42" pocket chart
* 8 sentence strips
* colored markers
* pictures for initial *y* and *z* words (See pages 106–107.)
* pictures for distracter words (Select pictures for other initial consonants.)
* poster paper
* crayons and paints

Getting Started

1. Write the poem above on sentence strips.

2. You may want to write each initial *y* and *z* in a second color.

3. Photocopy and color the pictures. Glue them onto cardstock and cut them out.

4. Write the following words on sentence strips, and cut into separate words:

yarn	yolk	yo-yo
zebra	zipper	zoo

Introducing the Poem

Place the sentence strips with the poem in the pocket chart, and read aloud the poem to children. Then ask children to read the poem aloud with you. Point out that this poem tells about two letters, *y* and *z*. Call on several volunteers to identify the words in the poem that begin with the /y/ sound and the letter *y*. (*you* in line 1; *yell* in line 3; *your* in line 4) Call on another volunteer to identify

the word that begins with the /z/ sound and the letter *z*. (*zoom* in line 3) Then explain that you will be showing them two pictures at a time. First they will identify the picture whose name begins with the /y/ sound made by the letter *y*; then they will identify the picture whose name begins with the /z/ sound made by the letter *z*.

Strengthening Phonics Skills

Place one initial *y* picture and one distracter picture below the poem. Call on a volunteer to say each picture name aloud, and identify the picture whose name begins with the /y/ sound. Remove the distracter picture and ask another volunteer to place the matching word strip (displayed on the chalkboard ledge) next to the picture. Continue until all three initial *y* pictures and words have been identified. Then follow the same procedure for the three initial *z* pictures and words. Ask children to come up with other initial *y* and *z* words on their own (for example: *year, yellow, yes, yesterday, yet, young, yogurt,* and *yummy; zip, zookeeper, zinc, zinnia, zone, zap, zucchini,* and *zillion*).

Finally, have children identify the rhymes in the poem. (*see* and *z*; *y* and *try*)

Going Beyond the Pocket Chart

Zany Movie Titles Explain to children that the word *zany* means *funny* or *silly*. Then invite them to make up zany movie titles in which at least one word begins with the letter *y* and one word begins with the letter *z*. Give examples, such as *The Yak and the Yellow Zucchini* or *A Zillion Zebras in My Yard*. Have children use poster paper, crayons, and paints to create colorful movie posters for their titles. Display them on a bulletin board titled "Zany Movies for You and Me!"

Short *a*

There are lots of **a**nimals in our world,

In lakes, in trees, on l**a**nd,

Th**a**t come in all shapes **a**nd sizes too,

Some small, some round, some gr**a**nd.

It's easy to think of **a**nimal names,

Like *fish*, **a**nd *bird*, **a**nd *hound*.

But c**a**n you think of **a**n **a**nimal name

Th**a**t h**a**s the short ***a*** sound?

⊛ MATERIALS ⊛

* 42" x 58" pocket chart or two smaller pocket charts
* 10 sentence strips
* colored markers
* pictures for short *a* words (See pages 108–109.)
* pictures for distracter words (Select animal pictures whose names have other short or long vowels, such as fox, pig, duck, whale, mule, hen, seal, and fish.)
* crayons
* drawing paper
* scissors

Getting Started

1. Write the poem above on sentence strips.

2. You may want to write the letter *a* that stands for the short *a* sound in a second color.

3. Photocopy and color the pictures. Glue them onto cardstock and cut them out.

4. Write the following words on sentence strips, and cut into separate words:

| cat | alligator | raccoon |
| parrot | camel | hamster |

Introducing the Poem

Place the sentence strips with the poem in the pocket chart. Read aloud the poem to children. Then invite children to read the poem with you. Explain that you are going to show them some pictures of animals. They will have to identify the animals whose names have the short *a* sound, /a/.

Ask children to point out all the words in the poem that have the short *a* sound. (*animals* in line 1; *land* in line 2; *that* and *and* in line 3; *grand* in line 4; *animal* in line 5; *and* in line 6; *can*, *an*, and *animal* in line 7; *that* and *has* in line 8)

Strengthening Phonics Skills ·············※

Use the short *a* pictures and distracter pictures to set up choice options that you think are appropriate for your children. For example, you may want to use one short *a* picture and one distracter picture, or one short *a* picture and two distracter pictures. Each time children identify a short *a* picture, ask them to find the corresponding word strip and place it beside the picture. Continue until all six pictures and words have been identified. Then encourage children to come up with short *a* animal words of their own (for example: *bat, clam, panda, badger, tadpole, panther, ant, jaguar, grasshopper,* and *rabbit*).

Finally, have children identify the rhyming words in the poem. (*land* and *grand*; *hound* and *sound*)

Going Beyond the Pocket Chart ···

Short *a* Animal Zoo Have children create a short *a* animal zoo on a bulletin board. First, have them draw and cut out a picture of an animal whose name has the short *a* sound. Then have them write a sentence about the animal that describes one of its attributes, using the following sentence starter: A *(name of animal)* has _____. For example, "A rabbit has long ears," or "A panda has black and white fur." Have them place their animal pictures and sentences on the bulletin board. Then invite them to decorate their zoo by adding features such as trees, ponds, and bridges.

Short *e*

What kinds of things

Would you like to s**e**ll—

Some **e**ggs, a sl**e**d, a j**e**t, or a b**e**ll?

Thinking of things isn't easy, you see,

Since what you s**e**ll

Must have the sound of short **e**!

○ MATERIALS ○

* ✳ 34" x 42" or 24" x 24" pocket chart
* ✳ 8 sentence strips
* ✳ colored markers
* ✳ pictures for short *e* words (See pages 110–111.)
* ✳ pictures for distracter words (Select pictures for short or long vowels.)
* ✳ pencils
* ✳ paper

Getting Started

1. Write the poem above on sentence strips.

2. You may want to write the letter *e* that stands for the short *e* sound in a second color.

3. Photocopy and color the pictures. Glue them onto cardstock and cut them out.

4. Write the following words on sentence strips, and cut into separate words:

dress	desk	shell
hen	net	bed

Introducing the Poem

Place the sentence strips with the poem in the pocket chart. Read aloud the poem, and invite children to read it along with you. Call on volunteers to find the words that have the short *e* sound, /e/. (*sell* in line 2;

eggs, *sled*, *jet*, and *bell* in line 3; *sell* in line 5) Then say: *Let's see how many other things we can name that have the short* e *sound!*

Strengthening Phonics Skills

Place a pile of 10 to 12 pictures near the pocket chart. The pile should contain the short *e* pictures as well as pictures whose names have other vowel sounds. In a separate pile, place the word strips for the short *e* words. Call on a volunteer to take a picture from the top of the pile and say its name. If the picture's name has the short *e* sound, such as *dress*, the child should place the picture and its corresponding word strip in the pocket chart. If the picture's name has another vowel sound, the child should put it aside. Continue until all pictures have been selected. Then challenge children to think of other short *e* words that name things they can sell (for example: *pet, pen, chess set, fence, belt, bench, kettle,* and *shelf*).

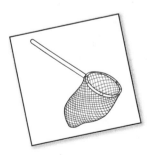

Finally, ask children to identify the rhymes in the poem. (*sell* and *bell*; *see* and *e*)

Going Beyond the Pocket Chart

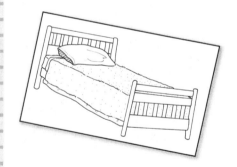

Sentences Have children choose one of the following groups of short *e* words, and write a sentence using at least two words from the group.

hen	met	yellow
pet	bed	rest
ten	red	best
tell	tent	went

Display children's work on a bulletin board with the title "Our Best Sentences for Short *e*."

Short i

Some folks like to make a list

Of things they need to buy,

Like grapes to munch and soup for lunch,

And a big blueberry pie!

Today we're going to make a list,

But the only words we'll supply,

Are words like *twig* or *pin* or *chimp*,

Which have the sound—short *i*!

MATERIALS

* 42" x 58" pocket chart or two smaller pocket charts
* 10 sentence strips
* colored markers
* pictures for short *i* words (See pages 112–113.)
* pictures for distracter words (Select pictures for other short or long vowels.)
* crayons
* drawing paper

Getting Started

1. Write the poem above on sentence strips.

2. You may want to write the letter *i* that stands for the short *i* sound in a second color.

3. Photocopy and color the pictures. Glue them onto cardstock and cut them out.

4. Write the following words on sentence strips, and cut into separate words:

ship	fish	mitt
bridge	crib	chick

Introducing the Poem

Place the sentence strips with the poem in the pocket chart, and read aloud the poem to children. Then ask children to join in and read the poem with you. Explain that today they will be making a list of words and pictures that have the short *i* sound that you hear in the word *list*.

Ask volunteers to say and point to the words in the poem that have the short *i* sound, /i/. (*list* in line 1; *big* in line 4; *list* in line 5; *twig*, *pin*, and *chimp* in line 7; *which* in line 8)

Strengthening Phonics Skills

Ask 10 children to come to the front of the room, and give each child a picture. Six children should have pictures for short *i* words. The rest should have pictures whose names have other short or long vowel sounds. Have each child, in turn, say the name of his or her picture. If a child has a picture whose name has the short *i* sound, such as *ship*, the child says: *I can add* ship *to our list*, and places the picture in the pocket chart. If a child has a picture whose name contains another vowel sound, such as *mop*, the child says: *I can't add* mop *to our list*, and places the picture on a table. After each child has had a turn, display the short *i* words on word strips. Call on volunteers to place the word strips next to their corresponding pictures. Then ask children to think of other short *i* words that can be added to the list (for example: *fin*, *bib*, *fig*, *gift*, *kiss*, *stick*, *six*, and *lips*).

Finally, have children identify the rhymes in the poem. (*buy* and *pie*; *munch* and *lunch*; *supply* and *i*)

Going Beyond the Pocket Chart

Wish Lists Distribute drawing paper to children, and invite them to complete the following sentence starter: *I wish _____*. Above their completed sentence, have them illustrate their wish inside a thought balloon. Display children's papers in columns on a bulletin board titled "Our Wish Lists."

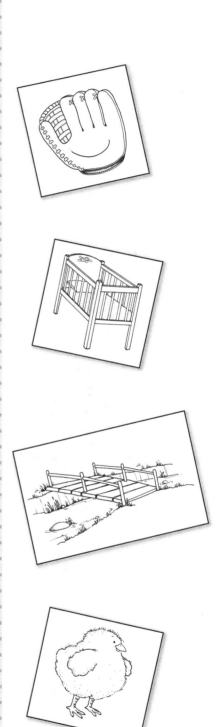

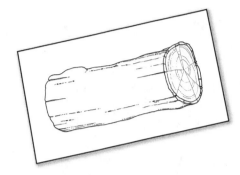

Short o

There are l**o**ts of things

You can put in a b**o**x,

Like a _____ and a _____,

And some bl**o**cks and your s**o**cks.

But each thing you put

In the b**o**x below,

Should have a name

With the sound of short **o**.

Getting Started

1. Write the poem above on sentence strips.

2. You may want to write the letter *o* that stands for the short *o* sound in a second color.

3. Photocopy and color the pictures. Glue them onto cardstock and cut them out.

4. Write the following words on sentence strips, and cut into separate words:

lock	log	clock
pot	top	mop

Introducing the Poem

Place the sentence strips with the poem in the pocket chart. Under the poem, place the shoebox. Read

aloud the poem to children. Then have children read the poem with you. Ask children how many blank spaces they see in the poem. (two) Explain that they will be filling each space with a picture and matching word that have the /o/ sound, which is the short *o* sound.

Ask children to find all the words in the poem that have the short *o* sound, /o/. (*lots* in line 1; *box* in lines 2 and 6; *blocks* and *socks* in line 4)

Strengthening Phonics Skills •••••••••••••• ✳

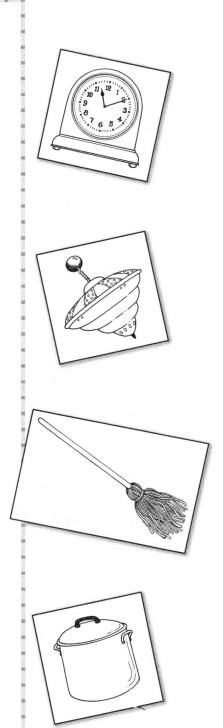

Use the short *o* pictures and distracter pictures to set up choice options that you think are appropriate for your children. You may want to use one short *o* picture and one distracter picture, or one short *o* picture and two distracter pictures. Whenever children place a short *o* picture in the poem, have them find the corresponding word strip (displayed on the chalkboard ledge), and place it beside the picture. Each time children complete the poem with two short *o* pictures and words, invite them to read aloud the poem. Then put the short *o* pictures and words in the box. Continue until all six words have been used to complete the poem. Then encourage children to come up with short *o* words of their own (for example: *rock, pond, pop, stop, knot, rod, hop, ox, cot,* and *dot*).

Finally, have children identify the rhymes in the poem. (*box* and *socks*; *below* and *o*)

Going Beyond the Pocket Chart

Box Sculpture Have children use boxes in different shapes and sizes to create a box sculpture. First, have them paint each box or cover it with decorative paper. Then have them draw a picture and/or write a word that has the short *o* sound on the sides of each box. Have students staple or tape the boxes together into an interesting shape to create a sculpture.

Short *u*

Under our umbrella
So pretty and new,
We will only place pictures
With the sound of short **u**.
How many can we find—
Two, three, maybe four?
No, I'm sure we can find
A whole lot more!

❂ MATERIALS ❂

❋ 42" x 58" pocket chart or two smaller pocket charts

❋ 12 sentence strips

❋ colored markers

❋ picture of a large umbrella

❋ pictures for short *u* words (See pages 116–117.)

❋ pictures for distracter words (Select pictures for other short or long vowels.)

❋ craft paper

❋ crayons

Getting Started ·············· ❋

1. Write the poem above on sentence strips.

2. You may want to write the letter *u* that stands for the short *u* sound in a second color.

3. Photocopy and color the pictures. Glue them onto cardstock and cut them out.

4. Write the following words on sentence strips, and cut into separate words:

brush	truck	drum
skunk	bus	cup

Introducing the Poem ········ ❋

Place the sentence strips with the poem in the pocket chart. Above the pocket chart, place the picture of the large umbrella that you have drawn and cut out. Read aloud the poem to children. Then ask children to read the poem along with you. Explain that you are going to show them some pictures of objects. They will identify the pictures that have the short *u* sound, /u/, that belong under the umbrella. Ask: *Do you hear the short* u *sound in the word* umbrella? *Where do you hear the sound? What letter makes the sound?*

Ask a volunteer to point to and say the two words in the poem that have the letter *u* that makes the /u/ sound. (*under* and *umbrella*)

Strengthening Phonics Skills

Use the short *u* pictures and distracter pictures to set up choice options that you think are appropriate for your children. For example, you may want to use one short *u* picture and one distracter picture, or one short *u* picture and two distracter pictures, or some other combination. Each time children choose a short *u* picture to place under the umbrella, have them find the corresponding word strip and place it next to the picture. Continue until all short *u* pictures and words have been placed under the umbrella. Then ask children to come up with other short *u* words on their own (for example: *fudge, cub,* and *plum*).

Finally, have children identify the rhymes in the poem. (*new* and *u; four* and *more*)

Going Beyond the Pocket Chart

A Rhyme Display the short *u* pictures and words in the pocket chart. Then write the following rhyme on sentence strips and place it in the pocket chart as well:

> **R**ub-a-d**u**b-d**u**b,
> Three _____ in a t**u**b.

Recall the familiar verse "Rub-a-dub-dub, three men in a tub" with children. Ask them to identify the words that have the short *u* sound. Then point to the incomplete verse in the pocket chart. Have children take turns completing the verse by adding an *s* to one of the short *u* words in the pocket chart or coming up with a word of their own.

Draw a picture of a large tub on a sheet of craft paper that covers a bulletin board. Invite children to draw their short *u* pictures in sets of three on the tub. The title of the bulletin board can be "**R**ub-a-d**u**b-d**u**b—Short *u* Pictures in Our Tub!"

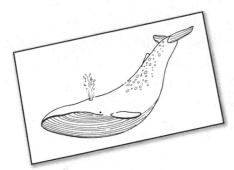

Long *a* (a-e)

I'll bring a g**a**m**e**.

She'll bring a fr**a**m**e**.

He'll bring a c**a**k**e**.

What will you t**a**k**e**?

I'll t**a**k**e** a _____.

MATERIALS

* 34" x 42" or 24" x 24" pocket chart
* 7 sentence strips
* colored markers
* pictures for long *a* words (See pages 118–119.)
* pictures for distracter words (Select pictures for other long or short vowels.)
* variety of pictures whose names have the long *a* sound
* pencils
* paper

Getting Started

1. Write the riddle above on sentence strips.

2. You may want to write each long *a* and silent *e* in a second color.

3. Photocopy and color the pictures. Glue them onto cardstock and cut them out.

4. Write the following words on sentence strips, and cut into separate words:

plate	plane	whale
cape	scale	cave

Introducing the Riddle

Place the sentence strips with the rhyming riddle in the pocket chart. Read aloud the riddle to children, and invite them to read it along with you. Explain that the answer to the riddle must be a word that has the /ā/ sound, which is the long *a* sound.

Call on volunteers to find all the words in the riddle that have the long *a* sound. (*game* in line 1; *frame* in line 2; *cake* in line 3; *take* in lines 4 and 5) Point out that all of these long *a* words follow the same pattern: The letter *a* is followed by a consonant and an *e*.

Strengthening Phonics Skills

Place a pile of 10 to 12 pictures near the pocket chart. The pile should contain the long *a* pictures, as well as pictures whose names have other long or short vowel sounds. In a separate pile, place the word strips for the long *a* words. Call on a volunteer to take a picture from the top of the pile and say its name. If the picture's name has the long *a* sound, such as *cape*, the child should place the picture and its corresponding word strip in the last sentence of the riddle and read it aloud: *I'll take a* cape. If the picture's name has another vowel sound, such as *desk*, the child should put it aside. Continue until all pictures have been selected. Then challenge children to think of other long *a* words to answer the riddle, in which the letter *a* is followed by a consonant and an *e* (for example: *vase, grape, lake, gate, rake, cage, cane, skate,* and *stage*).

Finally, have children identify the rhyming words in the riddle. (*game* and *frame*; *cake* and *take*)

Going Beyond the Pocket Chart

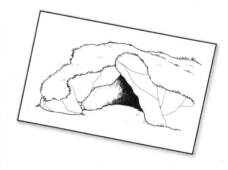

Make Up a Story Have children form small groups. Give each group several pictures whose names have the long *a* sound. Ask children to make up a story about the pictures. Be sure that each child in the group gets a turn to contribute to the story. Then have each group record its story and share it with the rest of the class.

Long *e (ea, ee)*

While sl**ee**ping under a tr**ee**,

I dr**ea**med about things with long **e**,

Like a _____ and a _____ and a str**ea**m,

And a bowl of chocolate ice cr**ea**m!

MATERIALS

* 34" x 42" or 24" x 24" pocket chart

* 6 sentence strips

* colored markers

* pictures for long *e* words (See pages 120–121.)

* pictures for distracter words (Select pictures for other long or short vowels.)

* drawing paper

* crayons

Getting Started

1. Write the poem above on sentence strips.

2. You may want to write the letters *ea* and *ee* in a second color.

3. Photocopy and color the pictures. Glue them onto cardstock and cut them out.

4. Write the following words on sentence strips, and cut into separate words:

peach	bee	sheep
deer	wheel	leaf

Introducing the Poem

Place the sentence strips with the poem in the pocket chart, and read aloud the poem to children. Then invite them to read the poem with you. Ask children how many blank spaces they see in the poem. (two) Explain that they will be filling each space with a picture and matching word that has the /ē/ sound, which is the long *e* sound.

Ask children to find all the words in the poem that have the long *e* sound. (*sleeping* and *tree* in line 1; *dreamed* in line 2; *stream* in line 3; *cream* in line 4) Point out that the letters *ea* and *ee* make the long *e* sound in these words.

Strengthening Phonics Skills

Place one long *e* picture and one distracter picture under the poem. Call on a volunteer to say aloud each picture name, and then identify the picture whose name has the long *e* sound. Ask the child to place the long *e* picture in one of the blank spaces in the poem. Then remove the distracter picture and ask another volunteer to find the corresponding word strip (displayed on the chalkboard ledge), and place it next to the picture. Repeat with another long *e* picture and distracter picture. Each time children complete the poem with two long *e* pictures and words, invite them to read aloud the poem. Continue until all six words have been used to complete the poem. Then challenge children to come up with their own words in which the letters *ea* and *ee* stand for the long *e* sound (for example: *peas, queen, meat, seal, feet, team, week, beach, wheat,* and *street*).

Finally, have children identify the rhymes in the poem. (*tree* and *e; stream* and *cream*)

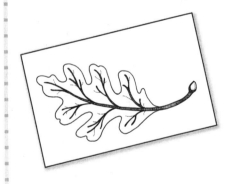

Going Beyond the Pocket Chart

Sweet Dreams Ask children to write a few sentences about a nice dream they've had, and then illustrate what their dream was about. Suggest that they draw a picture of themselves sleeping and then draw a picture of their dream inside a thought balloon. Display children's work on a bulletin board with the title "Sweet Dreams."

Long *i* (*i-e*)

Mike likes his new red bike.

He rides five miles a day.

And every time he rides a mile,

This is what he'll say:

"I know lots of long *i* words,

Like _____ and _____ and hike.

If you can say a long *i* word,

I'll let you ride my bike!"

MATERIALS

* 34" x 42" pocket chart
* 10 sentence strips
* colored markers
* pictures for long *i* words (See pages 122–123.)
* pictures for distracter words (Select pictures for other long or short vowels.)
* crayons
* drawing paper

Getting Started

1. Write the poem above on sentence strips.

2. You may want to write each long *i* and silent *e* in a second color.

3. Photocopy and color the pictures. Glue them onto cardstock and cut them out.

4. Write the following words on sentence strips, and cut into separate words:

hive	kite	tire
slide	pine	vine

Introducing the Poem

Place the sentence strips with the poem in the pocket chart, and read aloud the poem to children. Then

invite them to read the poem along with you. Ask children how many blank spaces they see in the poem. (two) Explain that they will fill each space with a picture and matching word that has the /ī/ sound, which is the long *i* sound. The long *i* words they will use will follow the same pattern: the letter *i* is followed by a consonant and an *e*.

Call on volunteers to find all the words in the poem that have the long *i* sound. (*Mike*, *likes*, and *bike* in line 1; *rides*, *five*, and *miles* in line 2; *time*, *rides*, and *mile* in line 3; *like* and *hike* in line 6; *ride* and *bike* in line 8) If children point out that the words *I*, *I'll*, and *my* also have a long *i* sound, compliment them on their listening skills. Explain that these words make the long *i* sound, but have different letter patterns.

Strengthening Phonics Skills

Give 10 children pictures. Six children should have pictures for the long *i* words. The rest should have pictures whose names have other long or short vowel sounds. Have each child, in turn, say the name of his or her picture. If a child has a picture whose name has the long *i* sound, such as *hive*, the child places the picture in one of the blank spaces in the poem. Then call on a volunteer to find the corresponding word strip (displayed on the chalkboard ledge), and place it next to the picture. If a child has a picture whose name has another vowel sound, such as *fish*, the child puts the picture aside. Each time children complete the poem with two long *i* pictures and words, invite the class to read aloud the poem. Continue until all six words have been used. Then challenge children to think of other long *i* words, in which the letter *i* is followed by a consonant and an *e* (for example: *life*, *fine*, *write*, *size*, *bite*, *side*, *hide*, *drive*, *rice*, and *prize*).

Finally, have children identify the rhyming words in the poem. (*day* and *say*; *hike* and *bike*)

Going Beyond the Pocket Chart

Big Smiles Ask children to draw a self-portrait with a big smile on their face. Beneath the portrait, have them write one or two sentences that tell about something or someone that makes them smile. Display children's work on a bulletin board with the following question as a heading: "What Makes Us Smile?"

Long o (o-e)

Take a cl**o**s**e** look

At h**o**m**e** and at school,

And you'll find th**o**s**e** words

That practice this rule:

An *o* plus a consonant

Trailed by an e

Makes the sound of long **o**,

I h**o**p**e** you agree!

MATERIALS

* 42" x 58" pocket chart or two smaller pocket charts
* 10 sentence strips
* colored markers
* pictures for long *o* words (See pages 124–125.)
* pictures for distracter words (Select pictures for other long or short vowels.)
* crayons
* drawing paper

Getting Started

1. Write the poem above on sentence strips.

2. You may want to write each long *o* and silent *e* in a second color.

3. Photocopy and color the pictures. Glue them onto cardstock and cut them out.

4. Write the following words on sentence strips, and cut into separate words:

nose	rope	cone
globe	hose	stove

Introducing the Poem

Place the sentence strips with the poem in the pocket chart. Read aloud the poem to children, and invite them to read the poem along with you. Call on volunteers to find the four words in the poem that have the /ō/ sound, which is the long *o* sound. (*close* in line 1; *home* in line 2; *those* in line 3; *hope* in line 8) Point out that all of these long *o* words follow the same pattern, which is described in the poem: the letter *o* is followed by a consonant and an *e*.

Tell children that they will look at some pictures and identify the ones whose names have a long *o* sound. Then they will come up with some long *o* words of their own.

Strengthening Phonics Skills

Use the long *o* pictures and distracter pictures to set up appropriate choice options for your children. You may want to place one long *o* picture and one distracter picture in the pocket chart, or one long *o* picture and two distracter pictures. Each time children identify the long *o* picture, ask them to find the corresponding word strip (displayed along the chalkboard ledge), and place it next to the picture. Continue until all six pictures and words have been identified. Then challenge children to think of other long *o* words, in which the letter *o* is followed by a consonant and an *e* (for example: *code, phone, broke, drove, zone, rode, froze, stone, vote,* and *spoke*).

Finally, have children identify the rhymes in the poem. (*school* and *rule; e* and *agree*)

Going Beyond the Pocket Chart

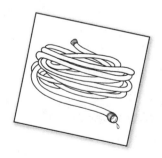

Telling Jokes Have children form pairs to think of one or two jokes or riddles to write down and then share with the class. Invite them to draw a picture that illustrates the punch line of their joke, as well. Display children's jokes and illustrations on a bulletin board with the heading "Telling Jokes Is Fun!"

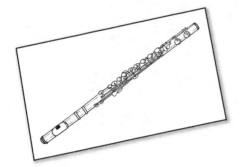

Long *u (u-e, ue)*

Please think of a word

With the sound of long **u**

That ends with an e,

Such as **u**s**e** and cl**ue**.

The word is _____.

❀ MATERIALS ❀

✳ 34" x 42" or 24" x 24" pocket chart

✳ 7 sentence strips

✳ colored markers

✳ pictures for long *u* words (See pages 126–127.)

✳ pictures for distracter words (Select pictures for other long or short vowels.)

✳ drawing paper

✳ crayons

✳ old magazines

Getting Started

1. Write the riddle above on sentence strips.

2. You may want to write each long *u* and silent *e* in a second color.

3. Photocopy and color the pictures. Glue them onto cardstock and cut them out.

4. Write the following words on sentence strips, and cut into separate words:

mule	flute	tube
cube	tune	glue

Introducing the Riddle

Place the sentence strips with the rhyming riddle in the pocket chart. Read aloud the riddle to children, and invite them to read it along with you. Explain that the answer to the riddle must be a word that has the /ū/ or /ü/ sound , which is the long *u* sound.

Call on volunteers to find the two words in the riddle that have the long *u* sound. (*use* and *clue* in line 4) Point out that in the word *use*, the letter *u* is followed by a consonant and an *e*, and in the word *clue*, the letter *u* is followed only by an *e*.

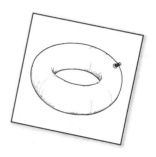

Strengthening Phonics Skills • • • • • • • • • ✷

Place a stack of 10 to 12 pictures near the pocket chart. The stack should contain the long *u* pictures, as well as pictures whose names have other long or short vowel sounds. In a separate stack, place the word strips for the long *u* words. Call on a volunteer to take a picture from the top of the stack and say its name. If the picture's name has the long *u* sound, such as *mule*, the child should place the picture and its corresponding word strip in the last sentence of the riddle and read it aloud: *The word is* mule. If the picture's name has another vowel sound, such as *nose*, the child should put it aside. Continue until all pictures have been selected. Then challenge children to think of other long *u* words that follow the pattern *u-e* or *ue* (for example: *June, rule, huge, rude, fuse, fume, blue, true, clue,* and *due*).

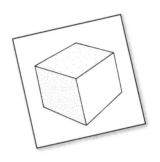

Finally, have children identify the rhyming words in the riddle. (*u* and *clue*)

Going Beyond the Pocket Chart

"What Is Cute?" Use the question "What is **cute?**" as a heading for a bulletin board. Ask children to answer the question by drawing a picture of something or someone they think is cute, or by cutting out a picture from a magazine. Below their picture, they should complete the following sentences:

I think _____ is (are) cute.

_____ is (are) cute because _____.

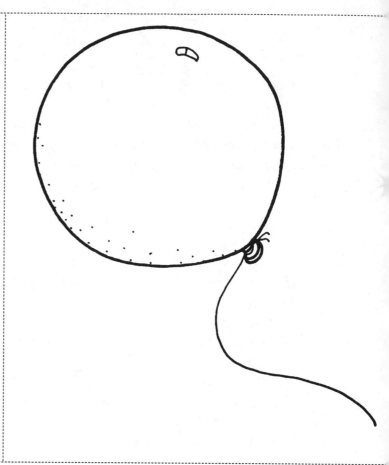

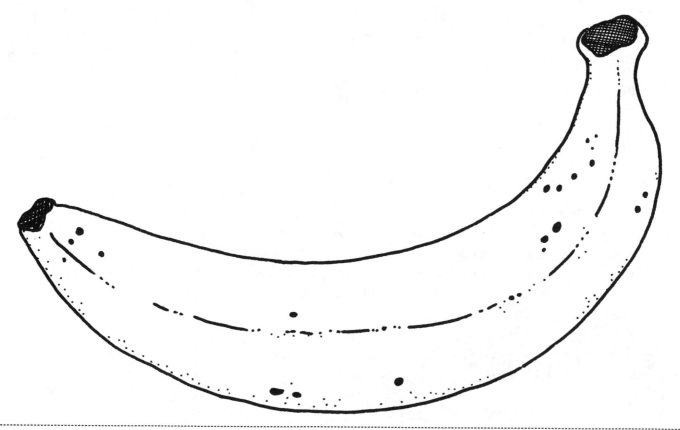

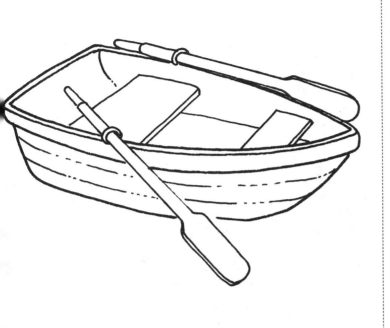

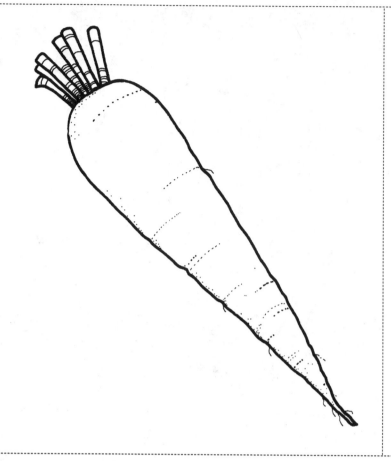

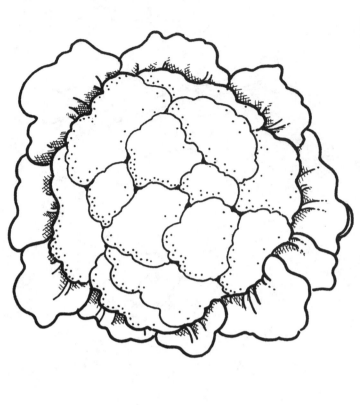

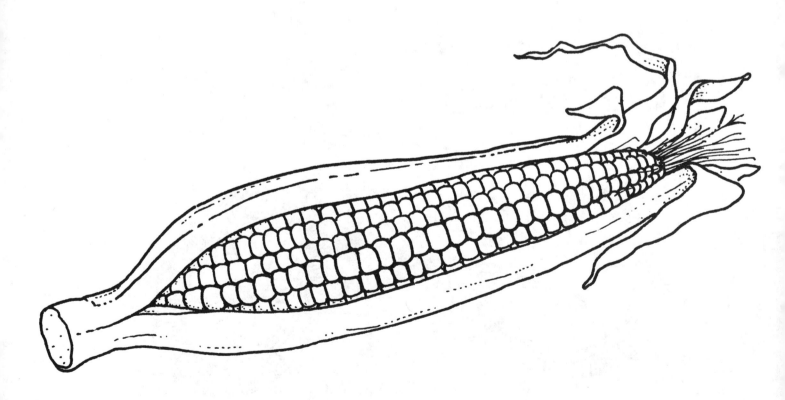

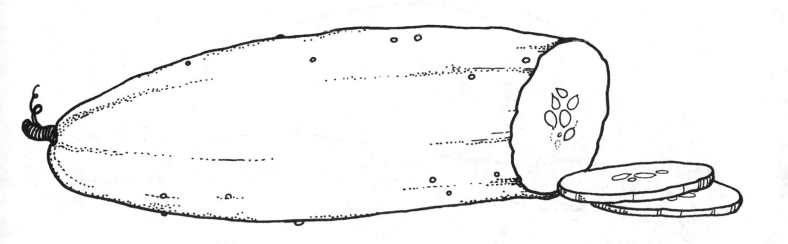

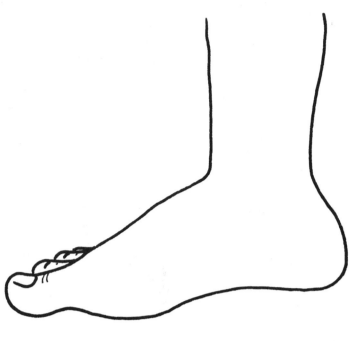

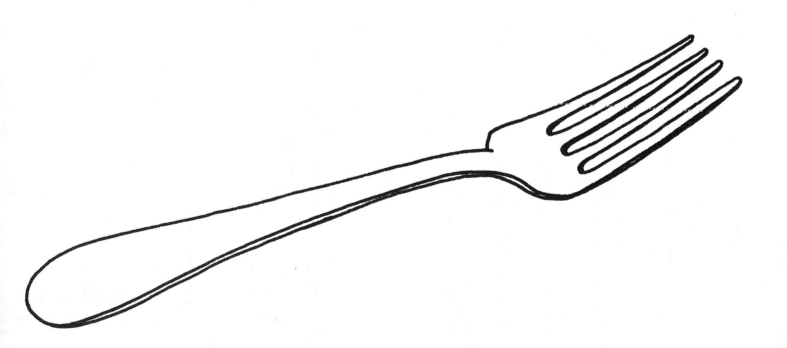

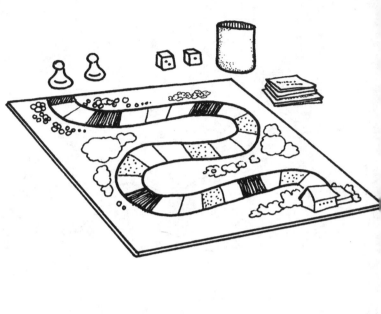

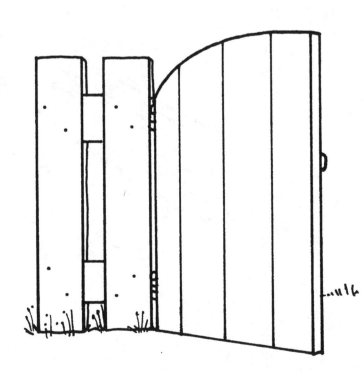

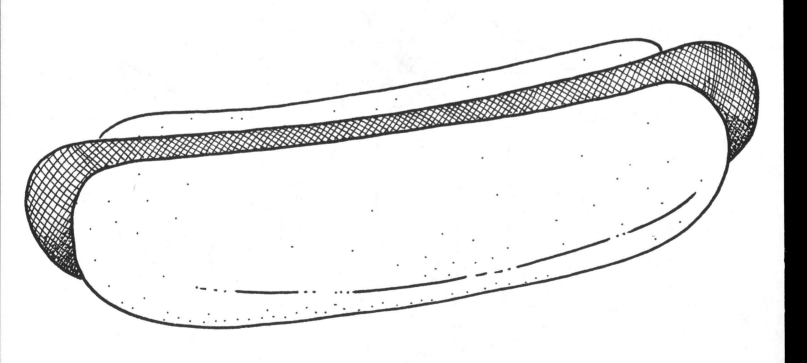

Initial *h*

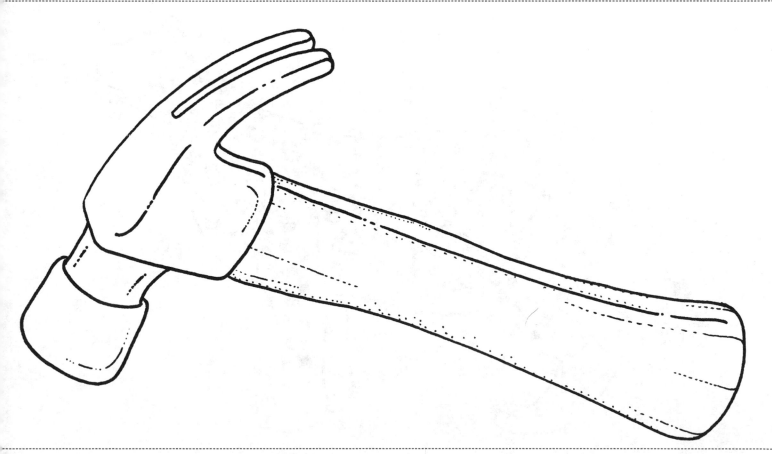

30 Pocket Chart Poems That Teach Phonics Scholastic Professional Books, page 79

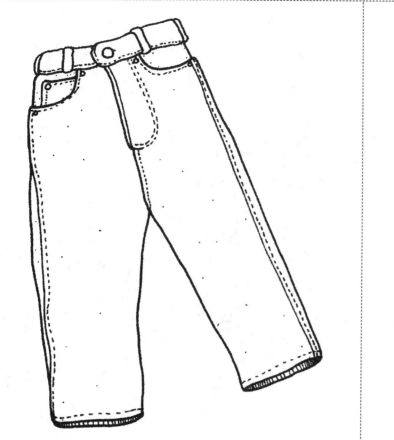

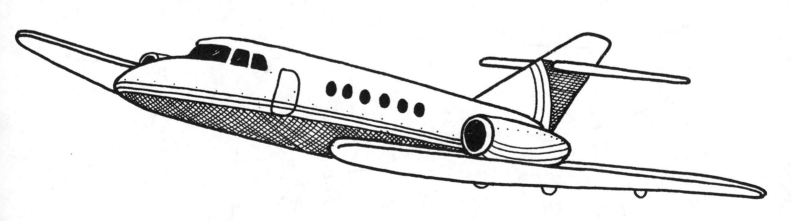

Initial *l*

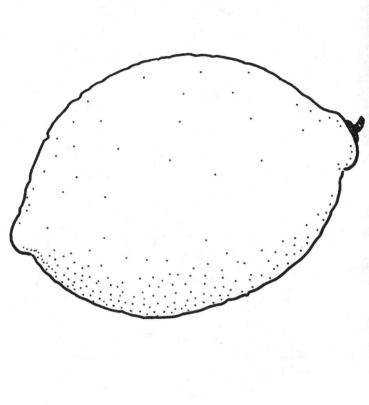

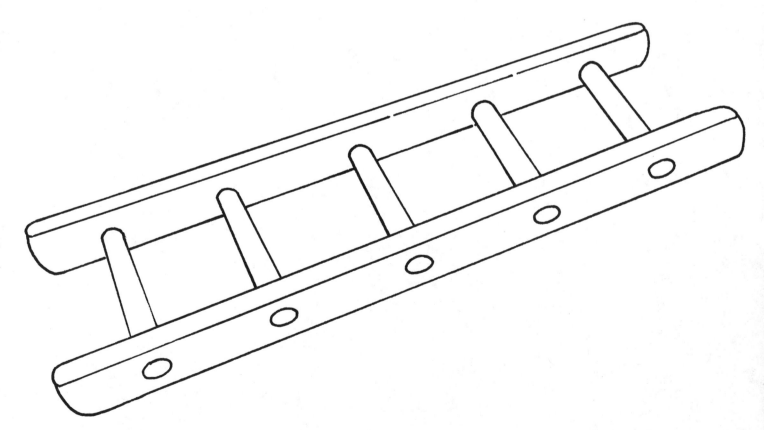

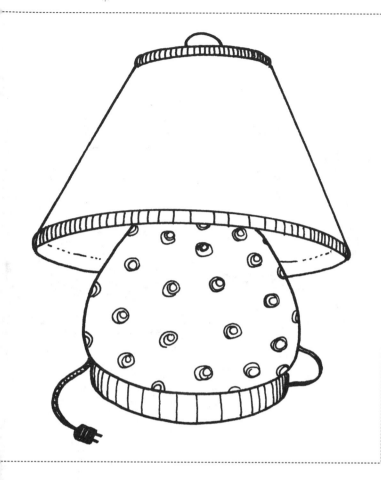

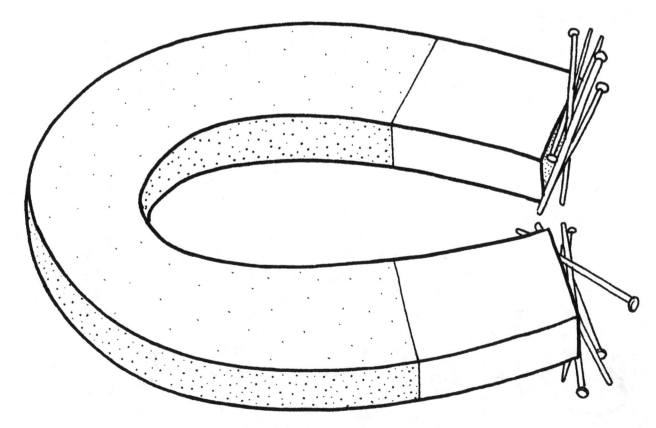

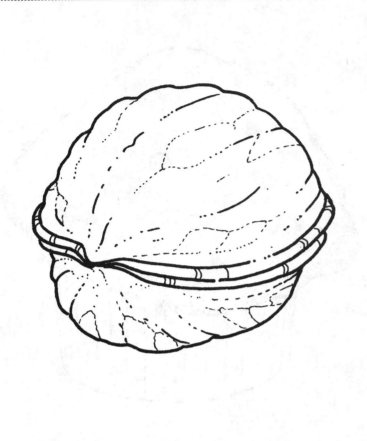

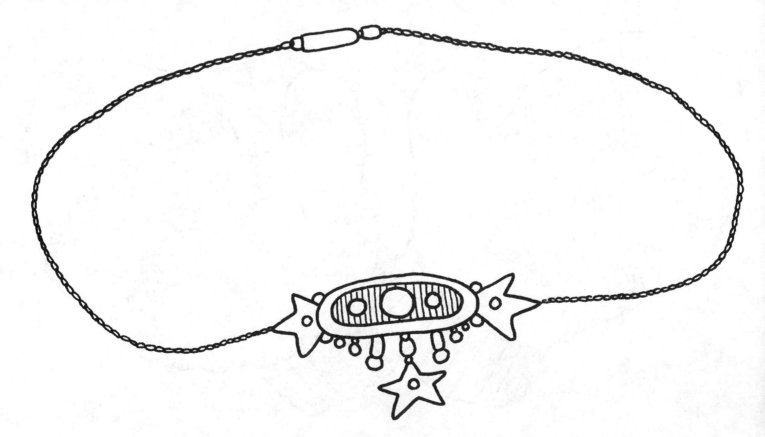

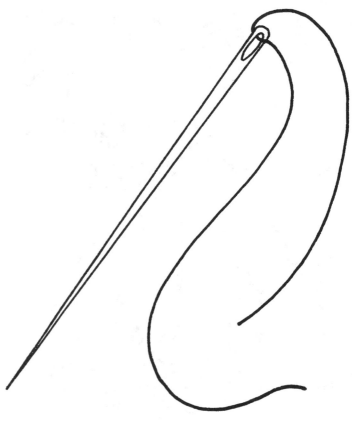

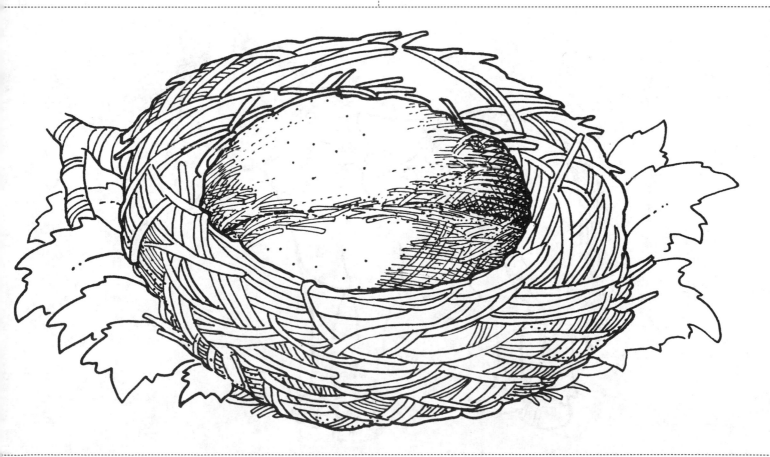

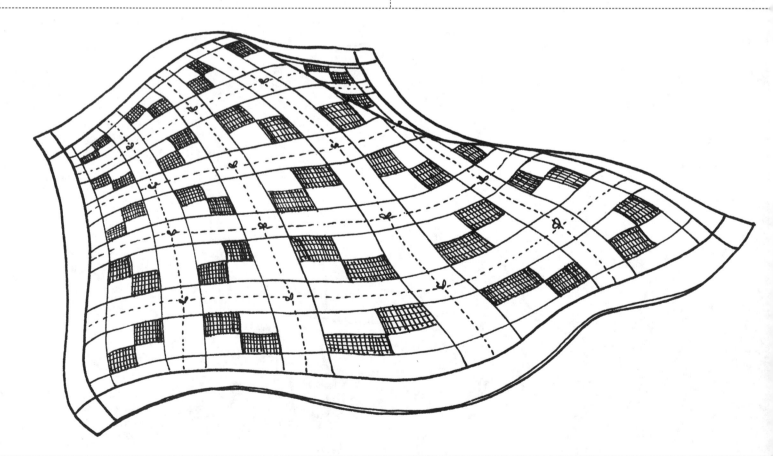

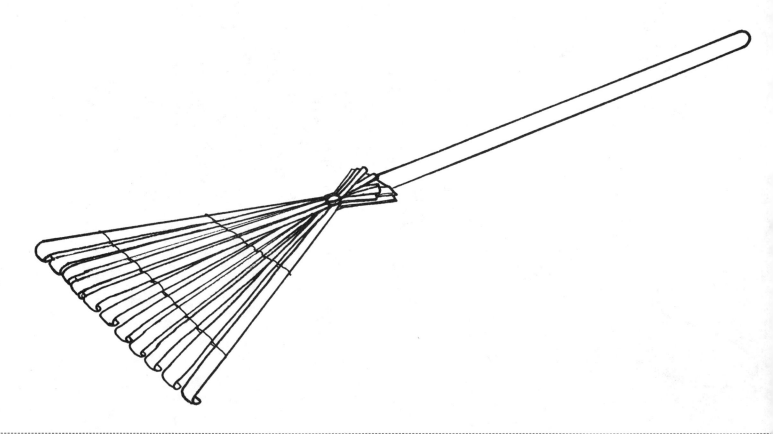

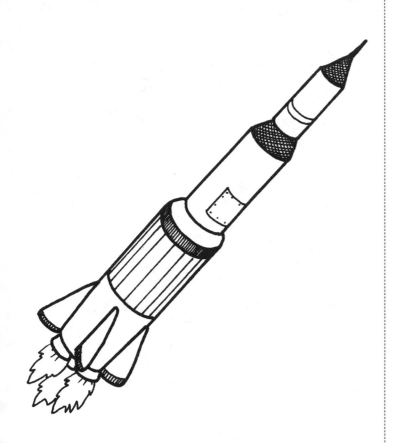

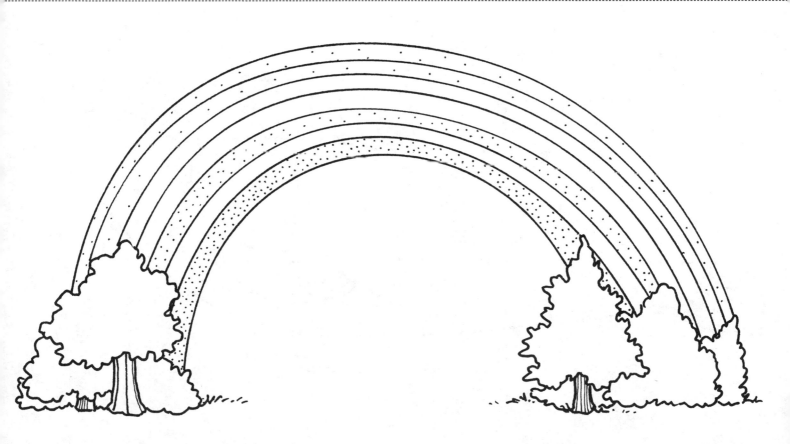

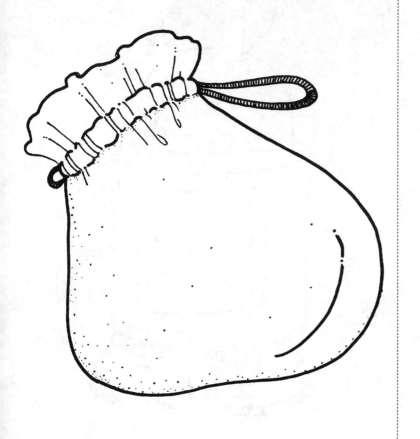

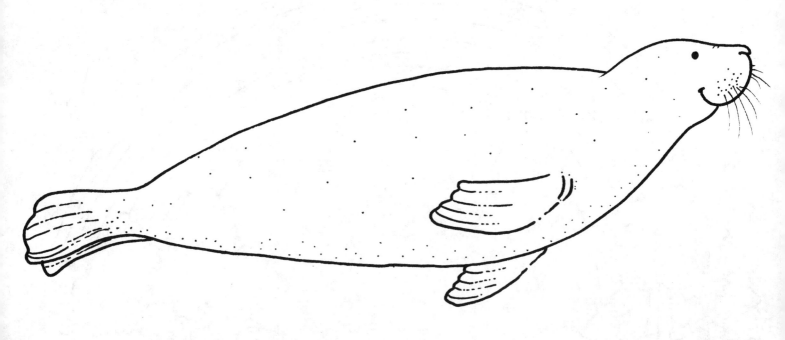

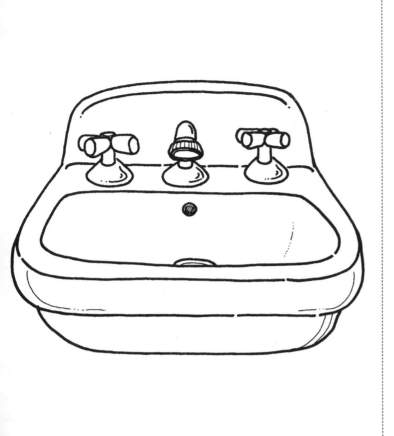

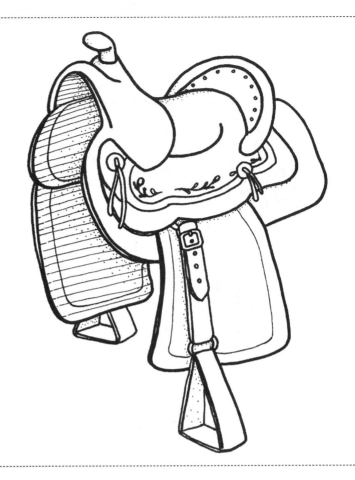

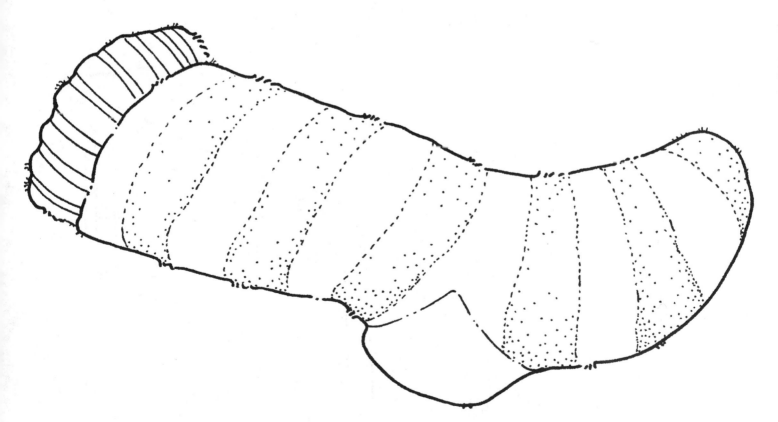

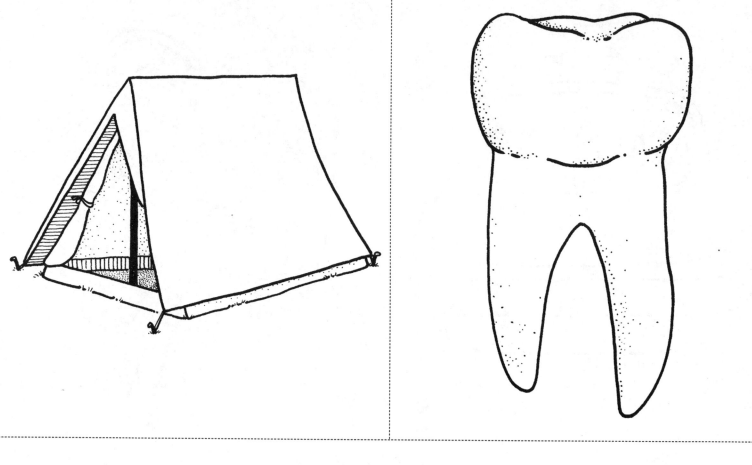

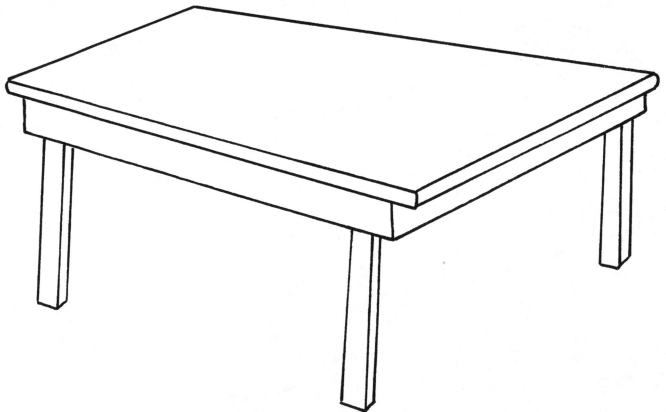

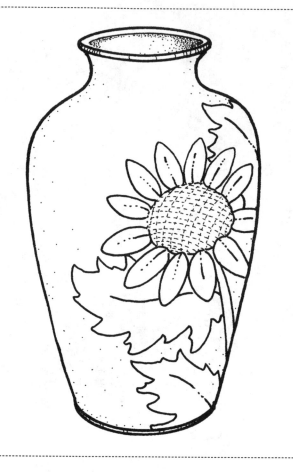

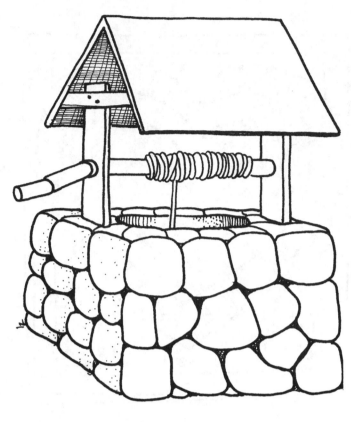

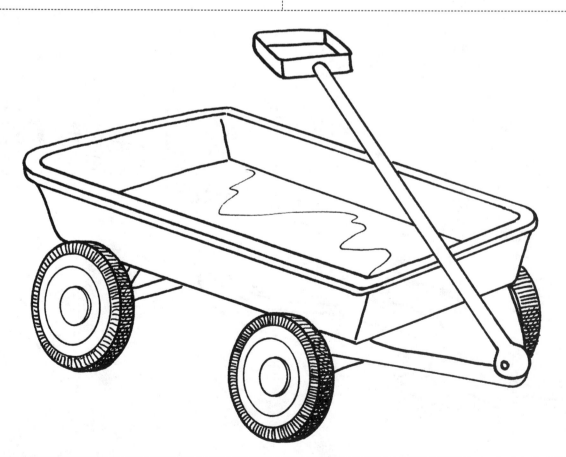

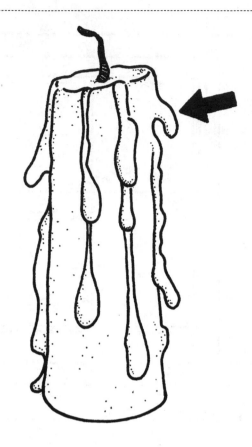

Final *x*

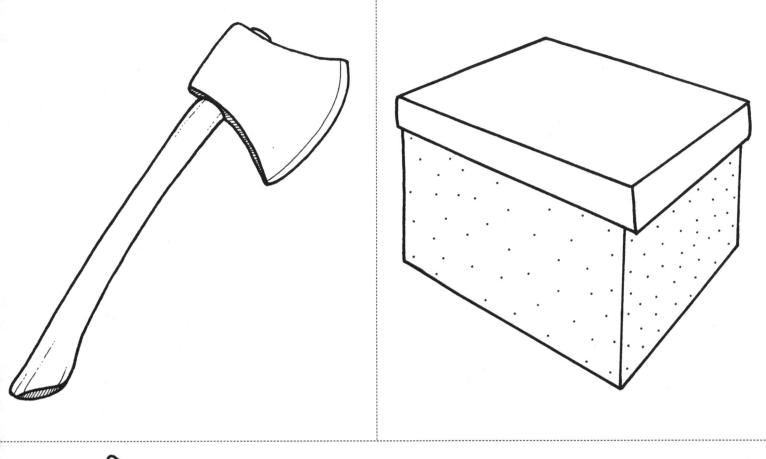

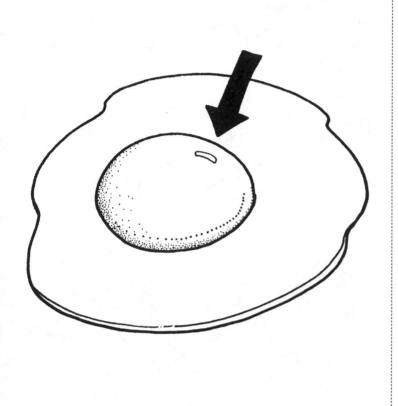

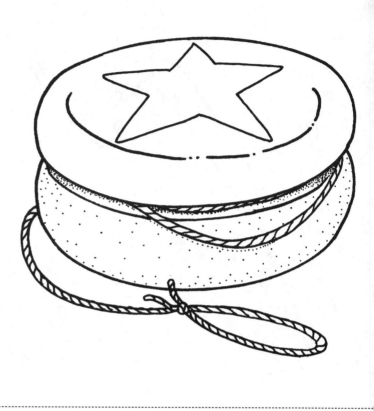

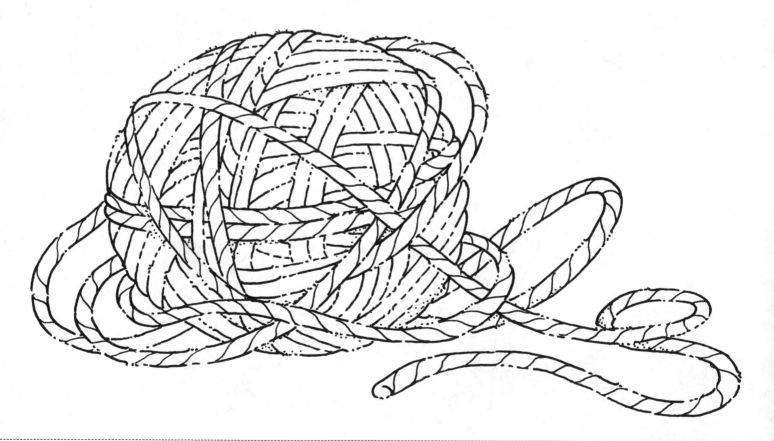

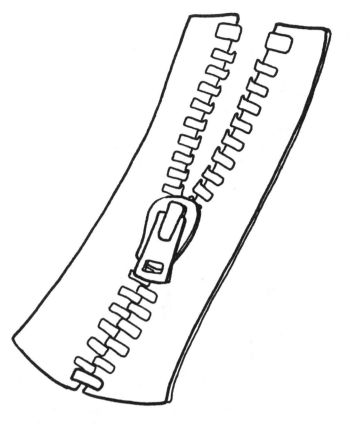

Short *a*

Short *e*

Short *e*

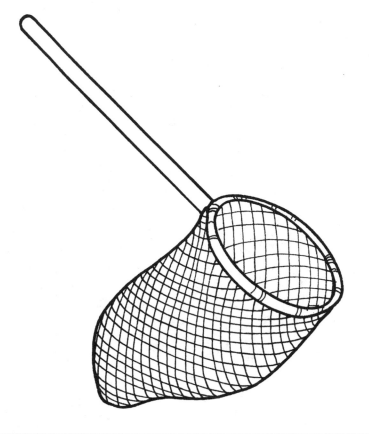

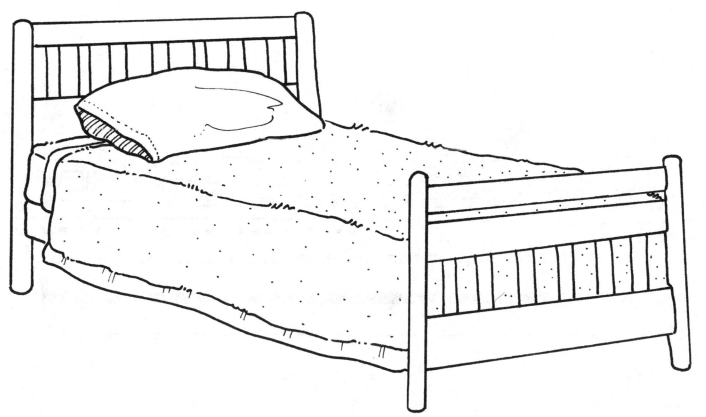

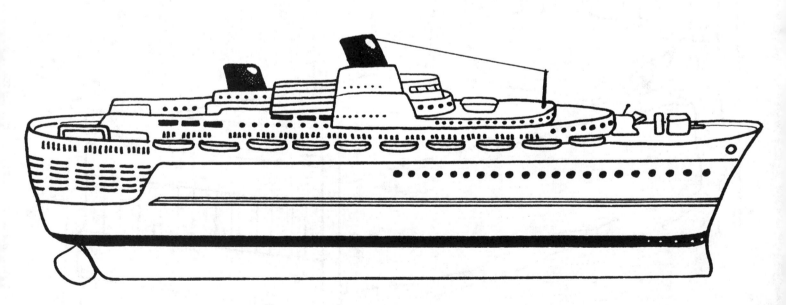

Short *o*

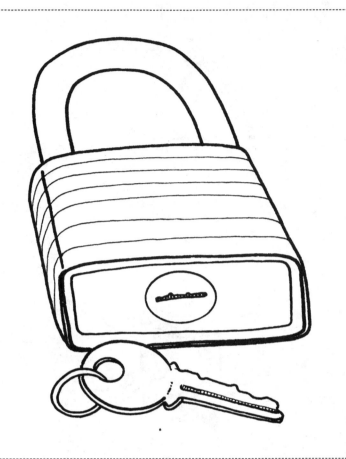

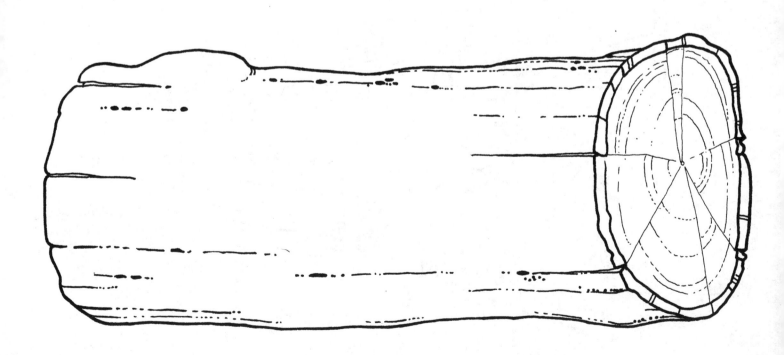

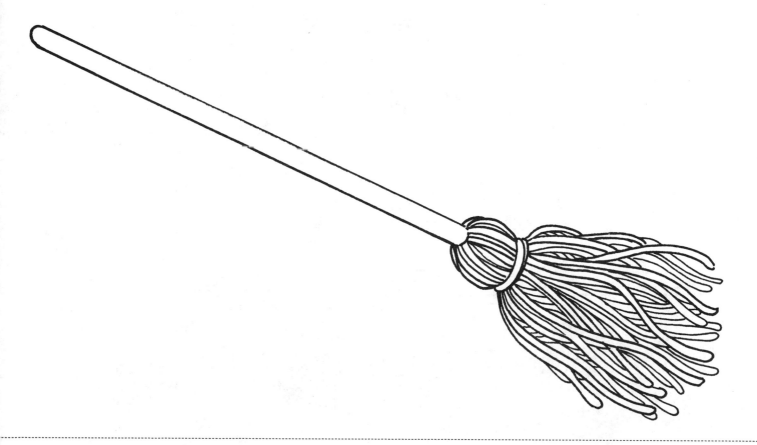

Short *u*

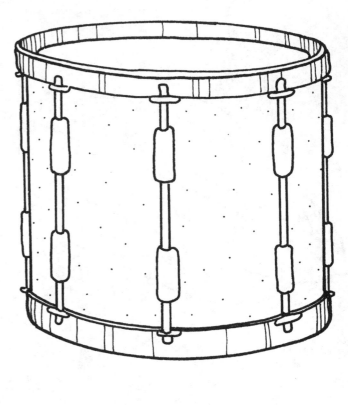

Short *u*

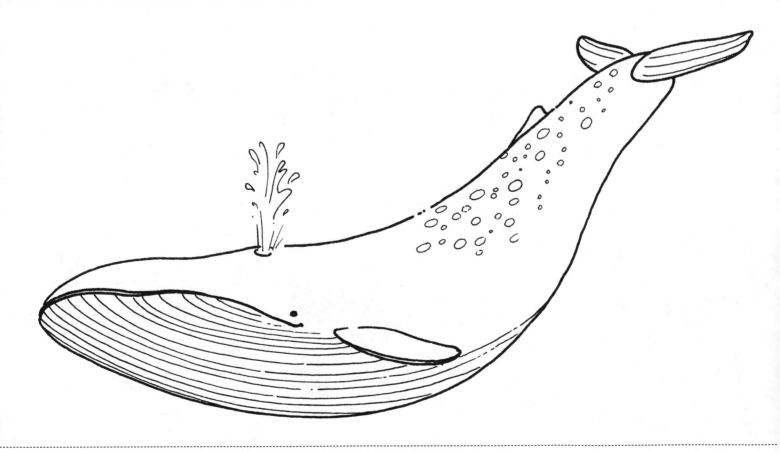

Long *a (a-e)*

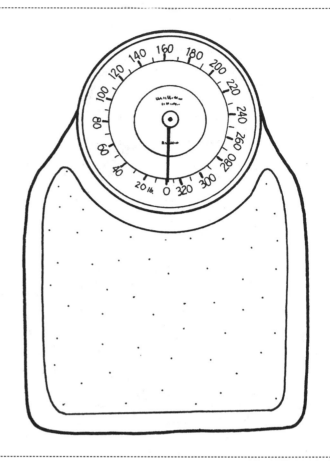

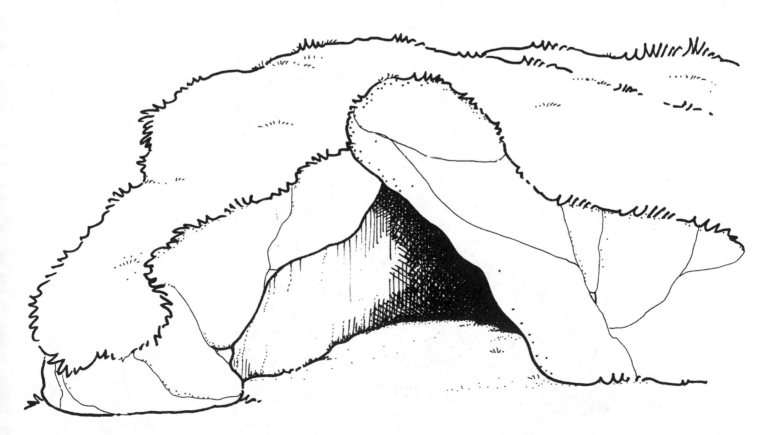

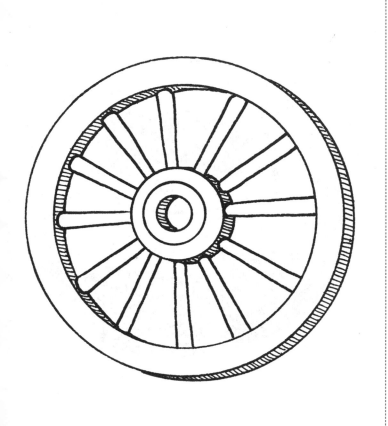

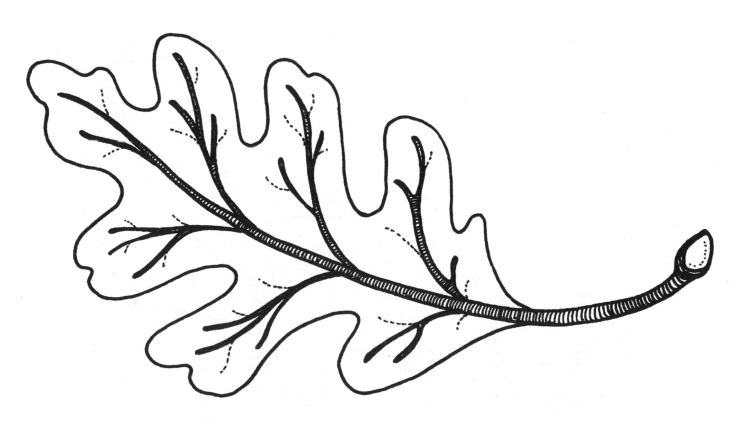

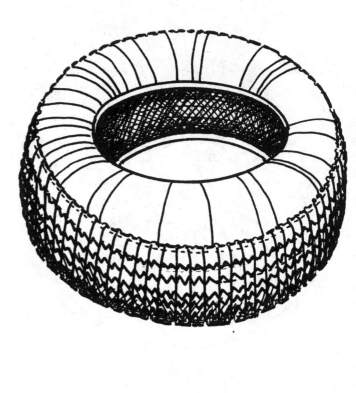

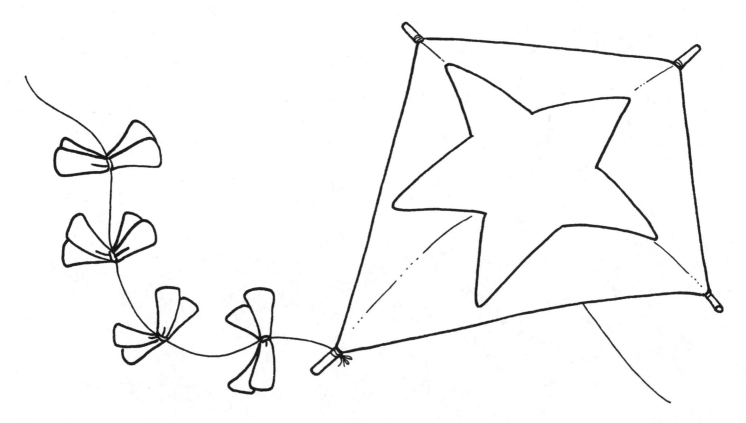

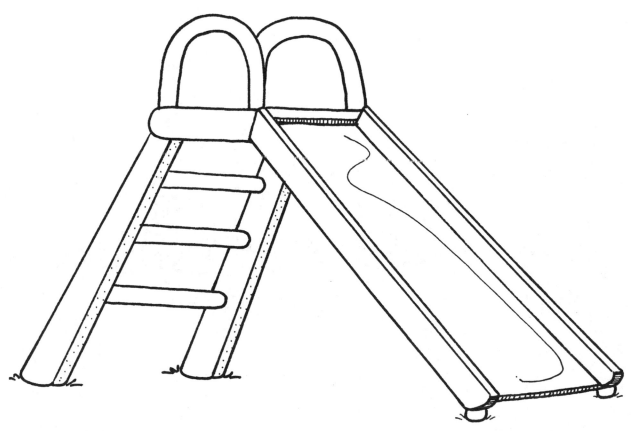

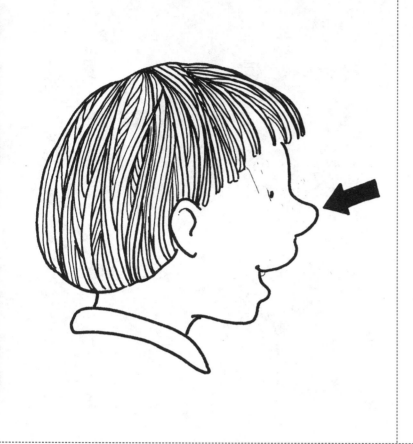

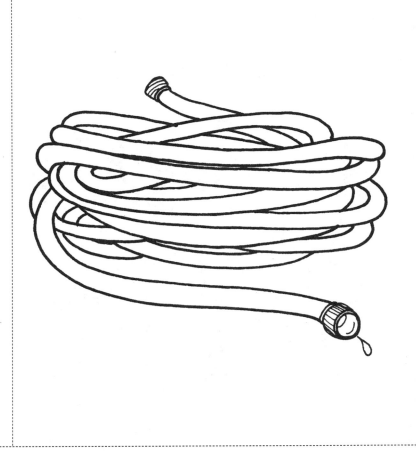

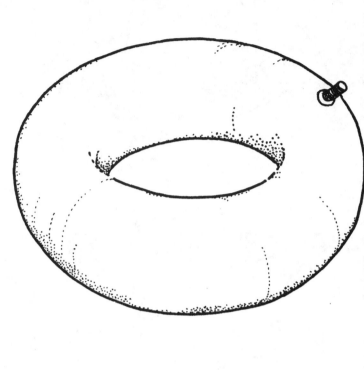

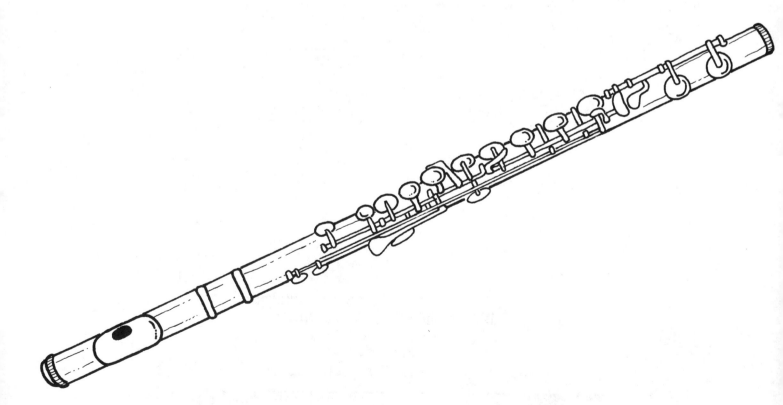

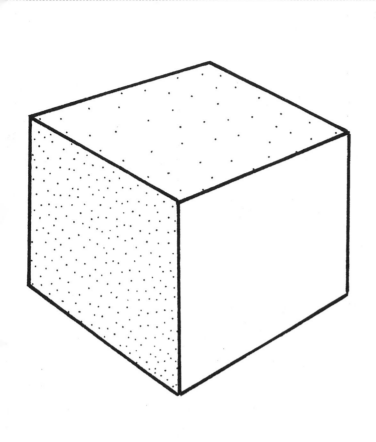

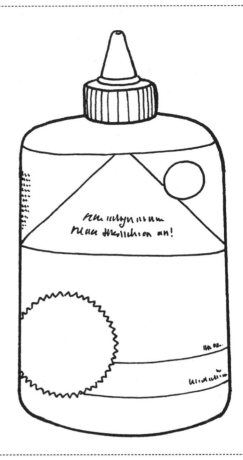

Notes